B R O A D W A Y   M U S I C A L S
Show by Show
1972-1988

W9-BPQ-664

C O N T E N T S

Hal Leonard Publishing Corporation
7777 West Bluemound Road P.O. Box 13819 Milwaukee, WI 53213

ISBN 0-7935-0782-0

Foreword

The Broadway musical, with its combination of music, dancing and visual delights, is truly one of America's great cultural treasures. From the hundreds of productions which have been mounted since 1891, we've selected the best music, and combined it with interesting facts and photographs to create a one-of-a-kind seven-volume songbook series: Broadway Musicals - Show By Show.

About The Author Of The Text

The comments about each show in this collection are excerpted from the book *Broadway Musicals Show by Show* by author Stanley Green. Mr. Green (1923-1990) was highly regarded as one of the leading scholars in the field of musical theatre. His eleven books are among the most widely read on the subject, including *The World of Musical Comedy, The Rodgers and Hammerstein Story, Broadway Musicals of the 30s, Starring Fred Astaire, Encyclopaedia of the Musical Theatre, Encyclopaedia of the Musical Film, The Great Clowns of Broadway, Broadway Musicals Show by Show,* and *Hollywood Musicals Year by Year.* He also compiled and edited *The Rodgers and Hammerstein Fact Book,* the definitive reference on that phenomenally successful collaboration.

Mr. Green was born in New York and lived there throughout his life. He began his writing career as a record reviewer for *Saturday Review,* and later was a contributing editor for *HiFi/Stereo Review.* His articles appeared regularly in such publications as *The New York Times, Musical America, Variety,* and *The Atlantic Monthly.* He worked as a film publicist in New York and London, and was public relations advisor to ASCAP for the years 1961-1965. In 1967 he wrote the script for the revue *Salute to the American Musical Theatre,* first performed at the Waldorf-Astoria, and subsequently presented at the White House on three consecutive evenings. He also wrote the script for "The Music of Kurt Weill" and was music advisor for "Review of Reviews," two programs presented at Lincoln Center in New York.

In 1974, at the request of Richard Rodgers, Mr. Green appeared with the composer on the first videotaped program for the Theatre Collection of the New York Public Library at Lincoln Center. He has been involved with many recording projects, including a 100-record series on Broadway musicals for the Franklin Mint, and the album *Starring Fred Astaire,* which he co-produced for Columbia. In 1987 he moderated a series of seminars marking the 100th birthday of George Abbott. Mr. Green presented many lectures on musical theatre and film at Union College, University of Hartford, New York University, C. W. Post College, Lincoln Center Library, Goodspeed Opera, and Marymount College. He continued to be active as a writer and researcher until the time of his death in December of 1990.

GREASE

Music, lyrics & book:
Jim Jacobs & Warren Casey

Producers:
Kenneth Waissman & Maxine Fox

Director: Tom Moore

Choreographer: Patricia Birch

Cast:
Adrienne Barbeau, Barry Bostwick,
Carole Demas, Timothy Meyers

Songs:
"'Summer Nights"; "Freddy, My Love";
"Greased Lightnin'"; "Mooning";
"Look At Me, I'm Sandra Dee";
"We Go Together";
"It's Raining On Prom Night";
"Beauty School Dropout";
"Alone At The Drive-In Movie";
"There Are Worse Things I Could Do"

New York run:
Eden Theatre, February 14, 1972; 3,388 p.

A surprise runaway hit, *Grease* opened at the Off-Broadway Eden Theatre (formerly the Phoenix), then moved on Broadway to the Broadhurst and then the Royale. And there it remained until April 13, 1980, for a record run that was not overtaken until *A Chorus Line* danced past the mark. The show, which began life as a five-hour amateur production in a Chicago trolley barn, took a satirically on-target view of the dress, manners, morals, and music of teenagers at the beginning of the rock and roll era. Set in the fictitious Rydell High School in Chicago, it is chiefly concerned with the attraction between greaser Danny Zuko (Barry Bostwick) and prim and proper Sandy Dumbrowski (Carole Demas), who eventually learns that there is little virtue in virtue. Mocking individuality and championing conformity, the musical hit a responsive chord in youthful audiences that could identify with teenagers having little on their minds except hanging out and making out. On Broadway, Danny was played by nine actors including Treat Williams. John Travolta, who was Danny in the 1978 movie opposite Olivia Newton-John, played Doody in the first of three touring companies.

DON'T BOTHER ME, I CAN'T COPE

Music, & lyrics: Micki Grant

Conception: Vinnette Carroll

Producers: Edward Padula & Arch Lustberg

Director: Vinnette Carroll

Choreographer: George Faison

Cast:
Alex Bradford, Hope Clarke,
Micki Grant, Bobby Hill,
Arnold Wilkerson

Songs:
"Don't Bother Me, I Can't Cope";
"Fighting For Pharaoh";
"Good Vibrations";
"It Takes A Whole Lot Of Human Feeling";
"Thank Heaven For You"

New York run:
Playhouse Theatre, April 19, 1972; 1,065 p.

A generally good-humored look at the social problems faced by black people today, *Don't Bother Me, I Can't Cope* was essentially a procession of musical numbers, both sung and danced, based on gospel, rock, calypso, and folk music. The show originated as a workshop project of Vinnette Carroll's Urban Arts Corps Theatre, after which it made appearances in Washington, Philadelphia, and Detroit before opening in New York at the Playhouse Theatre (on 48th Street east of 7th Avenue). Though stressing black pride and dignity, this "Musical Entertainment" still found room for some tongue-in-cheek self kidding which helped give it a broad enough appeal to keep it running on Broadway for two and one-half years.

3

A LITTLE NIGHT MUSIC

A Little Night Music. Len Cariou and Glynis Johns. (Martha Swope)

Music & lyrics:
Stephen Sondheim

Book:
Hugh Wheeler

Producer-director:
Harold Prince

Choreographer:
Patricia Birch

Cast:
**Glynis Johns, Len Cariou,
Hermione Gingold, Victoria Mallory,
Laurence Guittard, Patricia Elliott,
Mark Lambert, D. Jamin-Bartlett,
George Lee Andrews**

Songs:
**"Night Waltz";
"The Glamorous Life";
"Remember?";
"You Must Meet My Wife";
"Liasons";
"In Praise Of Women";
"Every Day A Little Death";
"A Weekend In The Country";
"It Would Have Been Wonderful";
"Send In The Clowns";
"The Miller's Son"**

New York run:
Shubert Theatre, February 25, 1973; 600 p.

*N*ot Mozart's K. 525 but Ingmar Bergman's 1955 film *Sommarnattens Leende (Smiles of a Summer Night)* was the inspiration for *A Little Night Music,* which offered a wry, witty view of a group of men and women from the standpoints of age and social position. The work claimed two musical innovations: the entire Stephen Sondheim score was composed in 3/4 time (or multiples thereof) and it had an overture sung by a quintet (whose members reappeared throughout the evening in the manner of a Greek chorus). It also contained, in "Send in the Clowns," the best known song the composer has written to date.

Taking place in Sweden at the turn of the century, the story deals with the complicated romantic world of a middle-aged lawyer, Fredrik Egerman (Len Cariou); his virginal child-bride Anne (Victoria Mallory); his son Henrik (Mark Lambert), who is in love with Anne; his former mistress, the actress Desirée Armfeldt (Glynis Johns); Desirée's current lover, the vain, aristocratic Count Carl-Magnus Malcolm (Laurence Guittard); and the count's suicidal wife, Charlotte (Patricia Elliott). The proper partners are paired off at a weekend at the country house of Desirée's mother (Hermoine Gingold), a former concubine of assorted members of the nobility. The musical toured for a year with Jean Simmons, Margaret Hamilton, and George Lee Andrews. A film version, in 1978, co-starred Elizabeth Taylor, Len Cariou, Diana Rigg, and Hermione Gingold.

A CHORUS LINE

Music:
Marvin Hamlisch

Lyrics:
Edward Kleban

Conception:
Michael Bennett

Book:
James Kirkwood & Nicholas Dante

Producer:
Joseph Papp for the
New York Shakespeare Festival

Director:
Michael Bennett

Choreographers:
Michael Bennett & Bob Avian

Cast:
Kelly Bishop, Pamela Blair,
Wayne Cilento, Kay Cole,
Patricia Garland, Baayork Lee,
Priscilla Lopez, Robert LuPone,
Donna McKechnie, Michel Stuart,
Thommie Walsh, Sammy Williams

Songs:
"I Hope I Get It";
"At The Ballet";
"Nothing";
"The Music And The Mirror";
"One";
"What I Did For Love"

New York run:
Public Theatre, April 15, 1975;
(still running 11/1/89)

*A*lthough it dealt with the hopes, fears, frustrations, and insecurities of a specific group of dancers auditioning for a chorus line, the musical skillfully conveyed the universal experience of anyone who has ever stood in line in an effort to present his or her qualifications for a job. Since that means just about all of us, *A Chorus Line* has managed to create such a strong empathetical bond with its audiences that it has become far and away the longest running production — musical or dramatic — ever staged on Broadway.

Director-choreographer Michael Bennett — who also receives program credit for having "conceived" the show — had long wanted to stage a work that would be a celebration of chorus dancers, known as "gypsies," who contribute so much and receive so little glory. Early in 1974, Bennett rented a studio where he invited 24 dancers to talk about themselves and their careers. Out of these rap sessions came some 30 hours of taped revelations, which gave the director the idea of creating his musical in the form of an audition. After he and Nicholas Dante, one of his dancers, had edited the tapes, producer Joseph Papp offered to sponsor the project as a workshop production at his New York Shakespeare Festival Public Theatre. Marvin Hamlisch and Edward Kleban were engaged to write the score, and playwright James Kirkwood was brought in to work with Dante on the book. The show opened at the Newman Theatre (part of the Public Theatre's complex) in mid April 1975, at a $10 top ticket price. Word of mouth made it a hit even before the critics were invited to view it on May 21, and it remained at the downtown playhouse for 101 performances. On July 25,1975, *A Chorus Line* moved to the Shubert Theatre, went on to win the Pulitzer Prize for drama, and — at this writing — it is still running on Broadway.

Avoiding a linear plot structure, the musical is basically a series of vignettes as 18 applicants vie for places in an eight-member chorus line. Goaded by a largely unseen — and rather sadistic — director named Zach (Robert LuPone), each applicant in turn reveals truths that, supposedly, will help the director make his final choices. Among those auditioning are Cassie (Donna McKechnie), a former featured dancer now down on her luck who was once romantically involved with Zach; the street-smart but vulnerable Sheila (Kelly Bishop) who recalls how she had been attracted to dancing because "everything was beautiful at the ballet"; the still-hopeful Diana (Priscilla Lopez), who had once failed a method acting class; the voluptuous Val (Pamela Blair) who uses silicone to enlarge her talent; and the pathetic Paul (Sammy Williams) who relates his humiliating experience as a drag queen.

There have been two touring companies of *A Chorus Line,* the first traveling for seven years, the second for five years eight months. The film version was released in 1985.

CHICAGO

Music:
John Kander

Lyrics:
Fred Ebb

Book:
Fred Ebb & Bob Fosse

Producers:
Robert Fryer & James Cresson

Director-choreographer
Bob Fosse

Cast:
**Gwen Verdon, Chita Rivera,
Jerry Orbach, Barney Martin,
Mary McCarty, M. O'Haughey,
Graciela Damiele**

Songs:
**"All That Jazz";
"All I Care About";
"Roxie";
"My Own Best Friend";
"Mr. Cellophane";
"Razzle Dazzle";
"Class";
"Nowadays"**

New York run:
46th Street Theatre, June 3, 1975; 898 p.

Chicago. Lawyer Jerry Orbach coaches murderess Gwen Verdon how to appear demure in the courtroom. (Martha Swope)

*B*ob Fosse first planned a musical production of Maurine Dallas Watkins' 1926 play as early as the mid-Fifties, with Gwen Verdon as the star and Robert Fryer as the producer. It took some 13 years, however, for him to clear the rights to the story of Roxie Hart, a married chorus girl who kills her faithless lover, avoids prison through the histrionic efforts of razzle-dazzle lawyer Billy Flynn (Jerry Orbach), and ends up as a vaudeville headliner with another "scintillating sinner," Velma Kelly (Chita Rivera). Though the show was a scathing indictment of American huckstering, vulgarity, and decadence, its atmosphere strongly recalled the Berlin of *Cabaret,* which also had songs by John Kander and Fred Ebb and whose film version was directed by Bob Fosse.

In Fosse's conceptual treatment, which had much in common with his *commedia dell'arte* approach in *Pippin, Chicago* was created as "A Musical Vaudeville" with a Master of Ceremonies introducing each number as if it were a variety act. (A previous effort to combine vaudeville within a musical play was the Kurt Weill-Alan Jay Lerner *Love Life.)* Soon after *Chicago's* Broadway opening, Miss Verdon was temporarily replaced by Liza Minnelli because of illness; during the run she was succeeded by Ann Reinking.

ANNIE

Music:
Charles Strouse

Lyrics:
Martin Charnin

Book:
Thomas Meehan

Producer:
Mike Nichols

Director:
Martin Charnin

Choreographer:
Peter Gennaro

Cast:
**Andrea McArdle, Reid Shelton,
Dorothy Loudon, Sandy Faison,
Robert Fitch, Barbara Erwin,
Raymond Thorne, Laurie Beechman,
Danielle Brisebois, Shelley Bruce**

Songs:
**"Maybe";
"It's The Hard-Knock Life";
"Tomorrow";
"Little Girls";
"I Think I'm Gonna Like It Here";
"N.Y.C.";
"Easy Street";
"You're Never Fully Dressed Without A Smile";
"Something Was Missing";
"I Don't Need Anything But You";
"Annie";
"A New Deal For Christmas"**

New York run:
Alvin Theatre, April 21, 1977; 2,377 p.

Annie. Annie (Andrea McArdle), Daddy Warbucks (Reid Shelton), and Sandy. (Martha Swope)

*T*he idea of turning Harold Gray's "Little Orphan Annie" comic strip into a musical was the inspiration of lyricist-director Martin Charnin, who then contacted playwright Thomas Meehan and composer Charles Strouse to join him in the project. Though their initial reaction was an unqualified "Ughhh," Meehan and Strouse were soon won over by Charnin's approach, which was to use only the three continuing characters in the strip — Annie, Daddy Warbucks, and Annie's mutt Sandy — and fit them into an original story. Because Meehan saw Annie as "a metaphorical figure standing for innate decency, courage and optimism in the face of hard times, pessimism and despair," he decided to set his fable in New York City in the midst of the Depression. Annie (Andrea McArdle), an 11-year-old foundling at the Municipal Orphanage, yearns for her parents to rescue her from the clutches of mean-spirited, bibulous Agatha Hannigan (Dorothy Loudon), the orphanage's matron. Presently, a miraculous parent-figure does show up in the person of billionaire Oliver Warbucks (Reid Shelton) whose secretary, Grace Farrell (Sandy Faison), has invited Annie to spend Christmas with him.

Annie. Orphans Diana Barrows, Robyn Finn, Donna Graham, Danielle Brisebois, Shelley Bruce, and Janine Ruane singing "You're Never Fully Dressed Without A Smile." (Martha Swope)

Warbucks, in fact, becomes so fond of the child that he plans to adopt her, a situation that is temporarily blocked by the machinations of Miss Hannigan. But the industrialist enlists the aid of his friend President Roosevelt (Raymond Thorne), and everyone — at least everyone who believes that tomorrow is only a day away — looks forward to having a New Deal for Christmas. (It should be noted that Lionel Bart's musical *Oliver!* is also about a young orphan who escapes a life of deprivation by being adopted by a wealthy gentleman.)

When tried out at the Goodspeed Opera House in Connecticut (where Miss McArdle replaced another girl shortly before the opening and Miss Loudon was not yet in the cast), *Annie* won the approval of Mike Nichols who offered to produce it on Broadway. The show was quickly adopted by theatregoers who made it the third longest running musical of the 1970s. During the run, Warbucks was also played by Keene Curtis, John Schuck, Harve Presnell, and Rhodes Reason; Annie by Shelley Bruce, Sarah Jessica Parker, Allison Smith, and Alyson Kirk; and Miss Hannigan by Alice Ghostley, Dolores Wilson, Betty Hutton, Marcia Lewis, Ruth Kobart, and June Havoc. There were four road companies of *Annie,* with the first traveling three and a half years. In 1982, the movie version was released with Albert Finney, Aileen Quinn, Ann Reinking, and Carol Burnett.

I'M GETTING MY ACT TOGETHER AND TAKING IT ON THE ROAD

Music:
Nancy Ford

Lyrics & book:
Gretchen Cryer

Producer:
**Joseph Papp for the
New York Shakespeare Festival**

Director:
Word Baker

Cast:
**Gretchen Cryer, Joel Fabiani,
Betty Aberlin, Don Scardino**

Songs:
**"Natural High";
"Miss America"; "Dear Tom";
"Old Friend"; "Strong Woman Number";
"Happy Birthday"**

New York run:
Public Theatre, June 14, 1978; 1,165 p.

*I*n all their works to date, composer Nancy Ford and lyricist-librettist Gretchen Cryer have been preeminently identified as feminist writers. *I'm Getting My Act Together and Taking It on the Road,* by far their most personal expression, even had the central role, that of a divorced 39-year-old pop singer attempting a comeback, played by Miss Cryer herself. The story finds her auditioning a new act for her dubious manager (Joel Fabiani), in which she presents herself as honestly as she can, without makeup or fancy gowns or any kind of audience-pandering. Through her songs, the singer gradually becomes the embodiment of the outspoken, totally liberated woman who knows exactly who she is and where she is going. After six months at the New York Shakespeare Festival Public Theatre, the musical was transferred to the Circle in the Square in Greenwich Village. During the run, Miss Cryer was succeeded by Virginia Vestoff, Betty Aberlin, Carol Hall, Betty Buckley, Anne Kaye, Nancy Ford, and Phyllis Newman.

THEY'RE PLAYING OUR SONG

Music: Marvin Hamlisch

Lyrics: Carole Bayer Sager

Book: Neil Simon

Producer: Emanuel Azenberg

Director: Robert Moore

Choreographer: Patricia Birch

Cast:
Lucie Arnaz, Robert Klein

Songs:
"Fallin'"; "If He Really Knew Me";
"They're Playing Our Song";
"Just For Tonight";
"When You're In My Arms"; "Right"

New York run:
Imperial Theatre, February 11, 1979; 1,082 p.

They're Playing Our Song was based in part on composer Marvin Hamlisch's own frequently stormy affair with his then lyricist-in-residence, Carole Bayer Sager. In this musical *drame à clef,* Vernon Gersch, a wise-cracking, neurotic songwriter who likes to spend his time telling his troubles to a tape recorder, and Sonia Walsk, a wise-cracking, neurotic lyric writer whose wardrobe is made up of used theatre costumes, try to have both a professional and a personal relationship despite constant interruptions caused by telephone calls from Sonia's former lover for whom she still feels great affection. To tell their story, the authors hit upon the notion — as in *I Do! I Do!* — of using only two characters, though in this case each one has three singing alter egos. Four actors succeeded Robert Klein during the Broadway run (including Tony Roberts and Victor Garber), and five succeeded Lucie Arnaz (including Stockard Channing and Anita Gillette). The show's first road company (with Garber and Ellen Greene) toured for two years; the second (with John Hammil and Lorna Luft) for one year three months.

EVITA

Music: Andrew Lloyd Webber

Lyrics: Tim Rice

Producer: Robert Stigwood

Director: Harold Prince

Choreographer: Larry Fuller

Cast:
Patti LuPone, Mandy Patinkin,
Bob Gunton, Mark Syers,
Jane Ohringer

Songs:
"On This Night Of A Thousand Stars";
"Buenos Aires";
"I'd Be Suprisingly Good For You";
"Another Suitcase In Another Hall;
"A New Argentina";
"Don't Cry For Me Argentina";
"High Flying Adored"; "Rainbow Tour";
"The Actress Hasn't Learned"; "And The
Money Kept Rolling In"; "Dice Are Rolling"

New York run:
Broadway Theatre,
September 25, 1979; 1,567p.

*B*ecause of its huge success in London (where it opened in 1978 and ran 2,900 performances), *Evita* was such a pre-sold hit in New York that it was able to surmount a mixed critical reception and remain on Broadway for three years nine months. Based on events in the life of Argentina's notorious Eva Peron, the musical — with Patti LuPone as Eva — begins in 1934 when Eva Duarte is 15, takes her from her hometown to Buenos Aires where she becomes a model, film actress, and the wife of Gen. Juan Peron (Bob Gunton). When Peron is elected president, Eva becomes the most powerful woman in South America, and though she does little to improve the conditions of her people, is regarded as a saint when she dies of cancer at the age of 33. Another character in the musical, the slightly misplaced Che Guevera (Mandy Patinkin), serves as narrator, observer, and conscience.

Though the plot is told entirely through song and dance (there is no credit for librettist) and the work had originated as a record project, the highly theatrical concept devised by authors Andrew Lloyd Webber and Tim Rice and director Harold Prince — as well as the popularity of "Don't Cry for Me, Argentina"— helped turn *Evita* into an internationally acclaimed musical. During the Broadway run, six actresses took over the title role from Miss LuPone: Terri Klausner, Nancy Opel, and Pamela Blake (matinees), and Derin Altay, Loni Ackerman, and Florence Lacey (evenings). The show's three touring companies traveled a total of three and one-half years.

Sweeney Todd

Music & lyrics:
Stephen Sondheim

Book:
Hugh Wheeler

Producers:
**Richard Barr,
Charles Woodward, Robert Fryer, etc.**

Director:
Harold Prince

Choreographer:
Larry Fuller

Cast:
**Angela Lansbury, Len Cariou,
Victor Garber, Ken Jennings,
Merle Louise, Edmund Lyndeck,
Sarah Rice**

Songs:
**"The Ballad Of Sweeney Todd";
"The Worst Pies In London";
"Johanna";
"Pretty Woman";
"Epiphany";
"A Little Priest";
"By The Sea";
"Not While I'm Around"**

New York run:
Uris Theatre, March 1, 1979; 557 p.

Sweeney Todd. Angela Lansbury and Len Cariou. (Martha Swope)

*E*asily the most grisly musical ever presented for a commercial Broadway run, the near-operatic *Sweeney Todd* was a bold, even audience-intimidating attack on the cannibalizing effects of the Industrial Revolution on a Brechtian, vermin-infestid London. The indictment was conveyed through the tale of a half-mad barber (Len Cariou) who returns home after escaping from an unjust imprisonment to take vengeance on the judge who sentenced him, then ravished his wife, and now plans to marry his daughter. But Sweeney doesn't limit himself to one victim; he turns his indiscriminate rage against everyone in London by systematically slitting the throats of his customers, whose corpses are then made into meat pies by Todd's enterprising accomplice, Mrs. Lovett (Angela Lansbury). At the end, of course, all the bad ones are properly and gruesomely punished.

First shown on the London stage in 1847 as *A String of Pearls,* or *The Fiend of Fleet Street,* by George Dibdin Pitt, the Grand Guignol story has been presented in many versions since then, most recently Christopher Bond's 1973 London play, *Sweeney Todd,* on which Hugh Wheeler based his libretto. The fifth and most uncompromising collaboration between composer-lyricist Stephen Sondheim and director Harold Prince, the production was also noted for its towering setting (by Eugene and Franne Lee) made from an iron foundry. During the run at the Uris Theatre (now the Gershwin, on 51st west of Broadway), Miss Lansbury was succeeded by Dorothy Loudon, Mr. Cariou by George Hearn. In 1984, the musical entered the repertory of the New York City Opera; in 1989, it was revived Off-Broadway with Bob Gunton and Beth Fowler.

CATS

Cats. "The Jellicle Ball" number. (Martha Swope)

Music:
Andrew Lloyd Webber

Lyrics:
Based on T.S. Eliot

Producers:
**Cameron Mackintosh,
Really Useful Co., Ltd., David Geffen**

Directors:
Trevor Nunn, Gillian Lynne

Choreographer:
Gillian Lynne

Cast:
**Betty Buckley, Rene Clemente,
Harry Groener, Stephen Hanan,
Reed Jones, Christine Langner,
Terrence V. Mann, Anna McNeely,
Ken Page, Timothy Scott**

Songs:
**"Jellicle Songs for Jellicle Cats";
"The Old Gumbie Cat";
"The Rum Tum Tugger";
"Old Deuteronomy";
"The Jellicle Ball";
"Grizabella";
"Macavity";
"Mr. Mistoffelees";
"Memory"**

New York run:
**Winter Garden, October 7, 1982;
(still running 11/1/89)**

---

*A*t this writing, *Cats* is still running in London (where it opened May 11, 1981) and in New York. Charged with incredible energy, flare, and imagination, the feline fantasy has been staged in its Broadway version as even more of an environmental experience than it was in its West End original. With the entire Winter Garden auditorium transformed into an enormous junkyard, a theatregoer is confronted by such sights as outsized garbagy objects spilling into the audience, a stage area without a proscenium arch, and a ceiling that has been lowered and turned into a twinkling canopy suggesting both cats' eyes and stars.

Composer Andrew Lloyd Webber began setting music to T.S. Eliot's poems in *Old Possum's Book of Practical Cats* in 1977. Later, he arranged the music for concerts, and still later — now in collaboration with director Trevor Nunn — he reworked the concept into a dramatic structure. In the song-and-dance spectacle, which has only the barest thread of a story line and no spoken dialogue, are such whimsically named characters as Jennyanydots (Anna McNeely), the Old Gumbie Cat who sits all day and becomes active only at night; the never satisfied Rum Tum Tugger (Terrence V. Mann); Bustopher Jones (Stephen Hanan), the well-fed, elegant cat about town; Mungojerrie and Rumpleteazer (Rene Clemente and Christine Langner), those two knockabout clowns and cat burglars; the patriarchal Old Deuteronomy (Ken Page); Skimpleshanks the Railway Cat (Reed Jones); and the mysterious Mr. Mistoffelees (Timothy Scott). The musical's song hit, "Memory," is sung by Grizabella (Betty Buckley), the faded Glamour Cat who, at the evening's end, ascends to the cats' heaven known as the Heaviside Layer. During the Broadway run (which saw ticket prices ascend from $40 to $55), Miss Buckley was succeeded by Laurie Beechman and Loni Ackerman. The first of three touring companies began traveling in December 1983.

LA CAGE AUX FOLLES

Music & lyrics:
Jerry Herman

Book:
Harvey Fierstein

Producer:
Allan Carr

Director:
Arthur Laurents

Choreographer:
Scott Salmon

Cast:
**George Hearn, Gene Barry,
Jay Garner, John Weiner,
Elizabeth Parrish, Leslie Stevens,
William Thomas Jr., Merle Louise**

Songs:
**"A Little More Mascara";
"With You on My Arm";
"Song On The Sand";
"La Cage aux Folles";
"I Am What I Am";
"Masculinity";
"The Best Of Times"**

New York run:
Palace Theatre, August 21, 1983; 1,176 p.

La Cage aux Folles. Les Cagelles. (Martha Swope)

*F*rench author Jean Poiret's successful play and film about the relationship between the owner of a St. Tropez drag-queen nightclub and his star attraction provided Broadway with its first homosexual musical. In the story, the flamboyant Albin (George Hearn) — known on the stage as Zaza — and the more conservative Georges (Gene Barry) are middle-aged lovers who have been together for over 20 years. Their domestic peace is shattered, however, when Jean-Michel (John Weiner), Georges' son as a result of a youthful indiscretion, advises his father that he plans to wed the daughter of Edouard Dindon (Jay Garner), a local morals crusader. In order that Georges appear to his future in-laws as an upstanding citizen, he agrees that Albin must somehow be put back into the closet. Though hurt and defiant ("I Am What I Am"), Albin swallows his pride and aids the deception by dressing up as Georges' wife. After inadvertently revealing that he is what he is, Albin is not above a little blackmail to force Dindon to permit the marriage to take place.

La Cage aux Folles. The "Masculinity" number with Gene Barry and George Hearn. (Martha Swope)

Except for the homosexual angle, *La Cage aux Folles* (the name of Georges' nightclub) was in the tradition of the big, splashy Broadway book musical, complete with a glamorous chorus line (which even has two female dancers among the Cagelles). And though it was originally to have been put together by a different team of collaborators (when it was known as *The Queen of Basin Street*), the musical was a predestined smash by the time of its Boston tryout. The show marked Jerry Herman's tenth score (as well as his first hit since Mame) and playwright Harvey Fierstein's first experience as a librettist. George Hearn, who scored a notable hit as Albin, was succeeded by Walter Charles and Keene Curtis; Gene Barry was followed by Jamie Ross, Keith Michell, Van Johnson, Steeve Arlen, and Peter Marshall. The show's two road companies were headed by, respectively, Michell (replaced by Barry) and Charles, and by Marshall and Curtis. *La Cage aux Folles* was the first musical to charge $47.50 for orchestra seats.

Male actors appearing in drag have long been part of the Broadway musical scene. In the late 19th Century, Tony Hart made a specialty of performing women's roles in Harrigan and Hart shows, and other early female impersonators were Julian Eltinge (the most celebrated of all) and Bert Savoy (of the team of Savoy and Brennan). Later actors who donned feminine attire — usually as a transvestite sight gag — included Ole Olsen in *Hellzapoppin*, Bobby Clark in *Mexican Hayride, Sweethearts,* and *As the Girls Go*, Ray Bolger in *Where's Charley?*, Myron McCormick in *South Pacific*, Bert Lahr (as Queen Victoria) in *Two on the Aisle*, Jack Gilford in *A Funny Thing Happened on the Way to the Forum*, Robrt Morse and Tony Roberts in *Sugar*, Mickey Rooney in *Sugar Babies*, and James Coco in the revival of *Little Me*. Actual homosexual — or at least effeminate — characters have been portrayed by Bobbie Watson in *Irene*, Danny Kaye in *Lady in the Dark*, Ray Bolger in *By Jupiter*, Joel Grey in *Cabaret*, Rene Auberjonois in *Coco*, Lee Roy Reams in *Applause*, Tommy Tune in *Seesaw*, and Michel Stuart and Sammy Williams in *A Chorus Line*.

THE TAP DANCE KID

Music: **Henry Krieger**

Lyrics: **Robert Lorick**

Book: **Charles Blackwell**

Producers:
**Stanley White, Evelyn Barron,
Harvey Klaris, Michael Stuart**

Director:
Vivian Matalon

Choreographer:
Danny Daniels

Cast:
**Hinton Battle, Samuel E. Wright,
Hattie Winston, Alfonso Ribiero,
Alan Weeks, Martine Allard, Jackie Lowe**

Songs:
**"Dancing Is Everything";
"Fabulous Feet";
"Class Act";
"I Remember How It Was" ;
"Dance If It Makes You Happy"**

New York run:
**Broadhurst Theatre,
December 21, 1983; 669 p.**

*T*he methods by which ambitious young blacks have been able to box or sing their way out of the ghetto have been documented in such musicals as *Golden Boy* and *Dreamgirls*, but *The Tap Dance Kid* offered the unaccustomed situation of an upper middle-class family in which a successful lawyer (Samuel E. Wright) tries to stifle the dreams of his ten-year-old son Willie (Alfonso Ribeiro) to follow the profession of his Uncle Dipsey (Hinton Battle) and become a dancer. Featuring Battle's exciting footwork, the show surmounted a divided press to chalk up a surprisingly long Broadway run. The musical's origin was a television play (in which librettist Charles Blackwell played the father) that had been based on a novel, *Nobody's Family Is Going to Change*, by Louise Fitzhugh.

BIG RIVER

Music & lyrics:
Roger Miller

Book:
William Hauptman

Producers:
**Rocco Landesman, Heidi Landesman,
Rick Steiner, M. Anthony Fisher,
Dodger Productions**

Director:
Des McAnuff

Choreographer:
Janet Watson

Cast:
**Rene Auberjonois, Reathal Bean,
Susan Browning, Patti Cohenour,
Gordon Connell, Bob Gunton,
Daniel H. Jenkins, Ron Richardson**

Songs:
**"Guv'ment";
"Muddy Water";
"River In The Rain";
"Waiting For The Light To Shine";
"Worlds Apart";
"You Ought To Be Here With Me";
"Leaving's Not The Only Way To Go"**

New York run:
**Eugene O'Neill Theatre,
April 25, 1985; 1,005 p.**

Big River. Ron Richardson and Daniel H. Jenkins.
(Martha Swope)

*P*roducers Rocco and Heidi Landesman came up with the idea of a musical version of Mark Twain's *Adventures of Huckleberry Finn* primarily because they were anxious to find the right property that would best introduce Broadway to the talents of country music songwriter Roger Miller. *Big River* was tried out at the American Repertory Theatre (ART) in Cambridge, Massachusetts, early in 1984, and then at the La Jolla Playhouse in California before those connected with the show felt that it was ready for New York. Set in 1849, with the action taking place both on the Mississippi River and in various locations along its banks (thanks to Heidi Landesman's atmospheric settings), the imaginative and faithfully conceived adaptation of the picaresque novel is concerned primarily with the relationship between Huck Finn and the runaway slave Jim (Daniel H. Jenkins and Ron Richardson) as they enjoy the untethered life traveling on a raft down the Mississippi from Hannibal, Missouri, to Hillsboro, Arkansas. In 1957, a previous musical based on Mark Twain's Mississippi River stories was offered Off Broadway under the title *Livin' the Life.*

SONG AND DANCE

Music:
Andrew Lloyd Webber

Lyrics:
Don Black, Richard Maltby Jr.

Adaptation:
Richard Maltby Jr.

Producers:
**Cameron Mackintosh,
Shubert Organization, FWM Producing Group**

Director:
Richard Maltby Jr.

Choreographers:
Peter Martins

Cast:
**Bernadette Peters, Christopher d'Amboise,
Gregg Burge, Charlotte d'Amboise,
Cynthia Onrubia, Scott Wise**

Songs:
**"Capped Teeth and Ceasar Salad";
"So Much To Do In New York";
"Unexpected Song";
"Come Back With The
Same Look In Your Eyes";
"Tell Me On A Sunday"**

New York run:
Royale Theatre, September 18, 1985; 474 p.

*T*he "Dance" of the title originated in 1979 when Andrew Lloyd Webber composed a set of variations on Paganini's A-Minor Caprice that seemed perfect for a ballet; the "Song" originated a year later with a one-woman television show, *Tell Me on a Sunday,* consisting entirely of musical pieces. Two years after that both works were presented together in London as a full evening's entertainment. In New York, this unconventional package won praise for Bernadette Peters, whose task in Act I was to create, without dialogue, the character of a freespirited English girl who has dalliances in America with four men. The second act offered a choreographic self-examination of one of the men (Christopher d'Amboise) and the two halves were joined when girl and boy were reunited. After a year on Broadway, Miss Peters was succeeded by Betty Buckley

ME AND MY GIRL

Music:
Noel Gay

Lyrics:
Douglas Furber, etc.

Book:
**L. Arthur Rose & Douglas Furber;
revised by Stephen Fry**

Producers:
**Richard Armitage, Terry Allan Kramer,
James Nederlander, Stage Promotions Ltd.**

Director:
Mike Ockrent

Choreographer:
Gillian Gregory

Cast:
**Robert Lindsay, Maryann Plunkett,
George S. Irving, Jane Connell,
Jane Summerhays, Nick Ullett,
Timothy Jerome, Thomas Toner,
Justine Johnston, Elizabeth Larner**

Songs:
**"Thinking Of No-One But Me";
"The Family Solicitor";
"Me And My Girl";
"Hold My Hand" (music with Maurice Elwin;
lyric: Harry Graham);
"Once You Lose Your Heart" (lyric: Noel Gay);
"The Lambeth Walk";
"The Sun Has Got His Hat On"
(lyric: Frank Butler);
"Take It On The Chin";
"Love Makes The World Go Round"
(lyric: Gay);
"Leaning On A Lamppost" (lyric: Gay)**

New York run:
**Marquis Theatre, August 10, 1986;
(still running 11/1/89)**

*O*ne of the most unlikely Broadway hits of 1986 was an almost fifty-year-old London musical comedy that, despite its near record-breaking run of 1,646 performances, had always been deemed too "English" to be considered for a New York showing before. Yet, followed by a successful West End reincarnation in 1985, *Me and My Girl* became an instant smash upon being offered as the premiere attraction at the newly built Marquis Theatre (located in the Marriott Marquis Hotel on Broadway between 45th and 46th Streets). Part of the reason had to do with the imaginative staging, Noel Gay's simple, catchy melodies, and the show's general spirit of eager-to-please innocent merriment. But most of the show's popularity surely was due to the protean talents of Robert Lindsay, the original star of the London revival who made his Broadway debut in the musical. (Lindsay was subsequently succeeded by Jim Dale and James Brennan.) The road company, which began touring in 1987, was initially headed by Tim Curry.

It was producer Richard Armitage, the son of the composer (Gay's real name was Reginald Armitage), who first saw the potential in bringing back *Me and My Girl.* The younger Armitage devoted years to tracking down the original score and script, then signed playwright Stephen Fry to do the text revisions with an assist from director Mike Ockrent. The book was still about a pugnacious Cockney, Bill Snibson (Lindsay), who turns up as the long-lost heir to the Earldom of Hareford. Complications arise over Bill's devotion to his Lambeth sweetie, Sally Smith (Maryann Plunkett), and the efforts of the Hareford clan (led by George S. Irving and Jane Connell) to send her back where she belongs. But the bluebloods—who even join in the high-strutting, thumb-cocking dance known as "The Lambeth Walk" — eventually give their consent and Bill ends up with both his inheritance and his girl (who has been miraculously transformed, *Pygmalion* fashion, into an elegant lady).

The character of Bill Snibson was originated in 1935 by the diminutive clown Lupino Lane in *Twenty to One,* a race-track yarn in which Bill tilts with the stuffy killjoys of the Anti-Gambling League. Lane became so attached to the part that two years later he had the show's librettists fashion a new musical for him about Bill's tilting with the stuffy members of the aristocracy. *Me and My Girl* was such a personal triumph that Lane toured in it extensively and brought it back to London in 1941, 1945, and 1949.

LES MISÉRABLES

Music:
Claude-Michel Schönberg

Lyrics:
Herbert Kretzmer

Conception:
Alain Boubil & Claude-Michel Schönberg

Original French Text:
Alain Boubil & Jean-Marc Natel

Adaptation:
Trevor Nunn & John Caird

Producer:
Cameron Mackintosh

Directors:
Trevor Nunn & John Caird

Choreographer:
Kate Flatt

Cast:
**Colm Wilkinson, Terrence Mann,
Randy Graff, Michael Maguire,
Leo Burmester, Frances Rufelle,
David Bryant, Judy Kuhn,
Jennifer Butt, Braden Danner**

Songs:
**"I Dreamed A Dream";
"Who Am I?";
"Castle On A Cloud";
"Master Of The House;
"Red and Black"
"Do You Hear The People Sing?";
"In My Life";
"On My Own"
(lyric with Trevor Nunn & John Caird);
"A Little Fall Of Rain";
"Drink With Me";
"Bring Him Home";
"Empty Chairs At Empty Tables"**

New York run:
**Broadway Theatre, March 12, 1987;
(still running 11/1/89)**

Les Misérables. Colm Wilkinson, Michael Maguire and David Bryant manning the barricade. (Michael Le Poer Trench/Bob Marshak)

*S*omething of a follow-up to the Royal Shakespeare Company's highly acclaimed non-musical dramatization of Charles Dickens' *Life and Adventures of Nicholas Nickleby, Les Miserables* was again directed by Trevor Nunn and John Caird, designed by John Napier, and lighted by David Hersey. (This time, however, it was produced by Cameron Mackintosh in partnership with the RSC.) Once more those responsible put together an epic saga dealing with the theme of social injustice and the plight of the downtrodden that had inspired the earlier massive 19th-century literary classic.

Originally conceived in 1979 by the French team of composer Claude-Michel Schönberg and lyricist Alain Boublil (with the collaboration of poet Jean-Marc Natel), the pop opera gives dramatic life to Victor Hugo's sprawling 1,200 page novel of suffering and salvation during a tumultulous period in French history. The story takes the valiant hero Jean Valjean from 1815 (after he has been paroled following 19 years on a chain gang for stealing a loaf of bread) to the illfated 1832 student uprising in Paris, when Valjean saves the life of Marius (David Bryant), the beloved of his adopted daughter Cosette (Judy Kuhn). Throughout the saga, Valjean is relentlessly hounded by the fanatic police inspector Javert (Terrence Mann) for breaking his parole, a pursuit that ends only when Javert, after chasing his quarry through the sewers of Paris, drowns himself in the Seine because he has violated his obsessive code of justice by letting Valjean escape.

With Herbert Kretzmer writing the English lyrics (and James Fenton credited for "additional material"), *Les Misérables* was successfully launched in London in 1985 at the RSC's Barbican Theatre, then brought to New York two years later by Mackintosh with the original lead, Colm Wilkinson, repeating his impressive performance as Valjean. (Wilkinson was subsequently replaced by Gary Morris, Timothy Shew, and William Solo.) Equally vital to the musical's appeal were Nunn and Caird's inventive, fluid staging and Napier's atmospheric sets — including an immense barricade for the uprising — that moved on a mammoth turntable. *Les Misérables* was the first musical in Broadway history to open at a top ticket price of $50.00. Prior to this production, the most successful musical of French origin (which also crossed the Atlantic via London) had been *Irma la Douce*.

STARLIGHT EXPRESS

Music:
Andrew Lloyd Webber

Lyricist:
Richard Stilgoe

Producers:
Martin Starger & Lord Grade

Director:
Trevor Nunn

Choreographer:
Arlene Phillips

Cast:
Ken Ard, Jamie Beth Chandler, Steve Fowler, Jane Krakowski, Andrea McArdle, Greg Mowry, Reva Rice, Robert Torti

Songs:
**"Rolling Stock";
"Engine Of Love";
"Pumping Iron";
"Make Up My Heart ;
"Starlight Express";
"I Am The Starlight";
"Only You" ;
"One Rock And Roll Too Many";
"Light At The End Of The Tunnel"**

New York run:
Gershwin Theatre, March 15, 1987; 761 p.

Starlight Express. The "Engine Of Love" number with Greg Mowry, Reva Rice, Jane Krakowski, Lola Knox (understudy for Jamie Beth Chandler), and Andrea McArdle. (© Martha Swope)

At a cost of well over $8 million — the highest in Broadway history — *Starlight Express* solidified the British invasion by joining *Cats, Me and My Girl,* and *Les Misérables* as one of the four biggest Main Stem attractions during the first half of 1987. Dubbed *Cats* on wheels, this hi-tech spectacle offered not only humanized railroad trains but put them on roller skates zooming on multilevel tracks around a glow-in-the-dark Erector-set panorama of the United States (created by John Napier), dominated by a gigantic steel suspension bridge that could turn, spin, dip and rise. The original idea for the fantasy began in 1973 when Andrew Lloyd Webber was asked to write a rock score for an animated television series based on the British equivalent of *The Little Engine That Could.* That never worked out but it started the composer thinking about a vaguely Cinderella-ish fable in which a battered steam engine named Rusty, encouraged by his father named Poppa, wins a race against a flashy diesel locomotive named Greaseball and a slick electric locomotive named Electra. First opening in London in 1984, the show itself became a flashy, slick hit (the original version offered skaters on ramps that encircled the theatre), then was reconceived for the American production requiring the renovation of the Gershwin Theatre (formerly the Uris) that alone cost $2.5 million.

THE PHANTOM OF THE OPERA

Music :
Andrew Lloyd Webber

Lyrics :
Charles Hart, Richard Stilgoe

Book:
Richard Stilgoe & Andrew Lloyd Webber

Producer:
**Cameron Mackintosh &
The Really Useful Theatre Co.**

Director:
Harold Prince

Choreographer:
Gillian Lynne

Cast:
**Michael Crawford, Sarah Brightman,
Steve Barton, Judy Kaye,
Cris Groenendaal, Nicholas Wyman,
Leila Martin, David Romano,
Elisa Heinsohn, George Lee Andrews**

Songs:
**"Think Of Me";
"Angel Of Music";
"The Phantom Of The Opera";
"The Music Of The Night";
"Prima Donna";
"All I Ask Of You";
"Masquerade";
"Wishing You Were Somehow Here Again";
"The Point Of No Return"**

New York run:
**Majestic Theatre, January 26, 1988;
(still running 11/1/89)**

The Phantom Of The Opera. Michael Crawford and Sarah Brightman. (Clive Barda)

*T*urn-of-the-century French novelist Gaston Leroux wrote *Le Fantôme de l'Opéra* after visiting the subterranean depths of the Paris Opera House — including its man-made lake. Though not a success when published in 1911, the ghoulish tale of the mad, disfigured Phantom who lives in the bowels of the theatre and does away with those who would thwart the operatic career of his beloved Christine, became internationally celebrated in 1925 when it served as a movie vehicle for Lon Chaney. (Subsequent film versions were made in 1943 with Claude Rains, in 1962 with Herbert Lom, in 1989 with Robert Englund, and—for television—in 1982 with Maximilian Schell.)

In 1984 a stage adaptation, using excerpts from public-domain operas by Verdi, Gounod, and Offenbach, was written and directed by Ken Hill and produced by Joan Littlewood at an East London fringe theatre. Andrew Lloyd Webber thought it might be developed into a campy West End musical — something along the lines of *The Rocky Horror Show* that he would co-produce with Cameron Mackintosh. After reading the Leroux novel, however, Lloyd Webber realized that far from being a penny dreadful, Leroux's work was a genuinely romantic and moving tale, and he decided to write the score himself. His lyricist and co-adapter was Richard Stilgoe and his director was Harold Prince. After a tryout of the first act at a summer festival at his home in Sydmonton (with Colm Wilkinson as the Phantom and Lloyd Webber's wife Sarah Brightman as Christine), the composer felt that there was need for a more romantic approach in the lyrics and, after first trying to enlist Alan Jay Lerner and then Tim Rice, he settled on the relatively inexperienced Charles Hart to augment Stilgoe's work.

The Phantom of the Opera opened in London in 1986 with Michael Crawford and Miss Brightman. It won a resoundingly affirmative reception for its cast, staging, and scenic effects, including a chandelier that descends from the auditorium ceiling and crashes on stage. At this writing, the musical is still running at Her Majesty's Theatre. Basically the same production was transferred to Broadway, with Crawford, Miss Brightman, and Steve Barton (as The Phantom's romantic rival) repeating their roles. A presold hit with an $18 million advance, the show made Andrew Lloyd Webber the first composer to have three musicals running simultaneously in London and New York. (The other two: *Cats,* and *Starlight Express.)*

So far during the Broadway run, Crawford has been succeeded by Timothy Nolen and Cris Groenendaal; Miss Brightman by Patti Cohenour and Rebecca Luker; Barton by Kevin Gray; and Judy Kaye by Marilyn Caskey. Two road companies opened in 1989: the first, in Los Angeles, had a cast headed by Crawford, Dale Kristien, Reece Holland, and Leigh Munro; the second, in Toronto, featured Colm Wilkinson, Rebecca Caine, Byron Nease, and Lyse Guerin.

THANK HEAVEN FOR YOU
(From "DON'T BOTHER ME, I CAN'T COPE")

Moderately slow

Words and Music by MICKI GRANT

Summer Nights

Lyric and Music by WARREN CASEY
and JIM JACOBS

uh. Tell me more. Tell me more. Did you get ver-y far?___ Tell me more. Tell me more. Like, does he have a car?
uh. Tell me more. Tell me more. Was it love at first sight?___ Tell me more. Tell me more. Did she put up a fight?

uh, oh, those Sum-mer Nights.___

Tell me more, tell me more. But you don't got to brag.___ Tell me more, tell me more. 'Cause he sounds like a drag.___

Shu-da bop bop. Shu-da bop bop. Shu-da bop bop. Shu-da bop bop. Girl: "He got friend-ly,

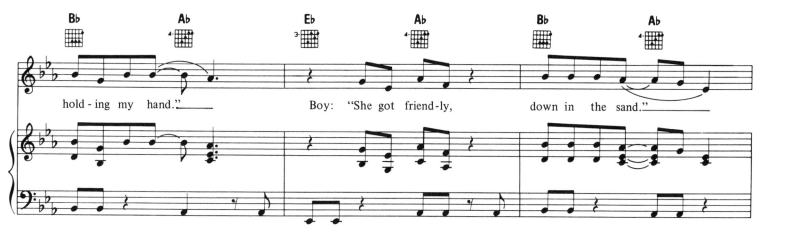

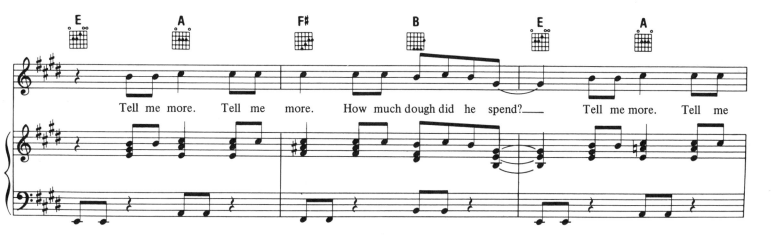

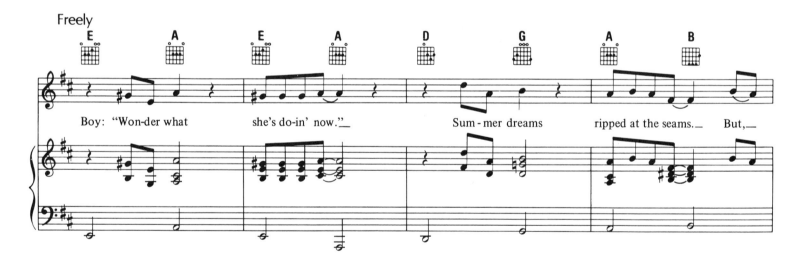

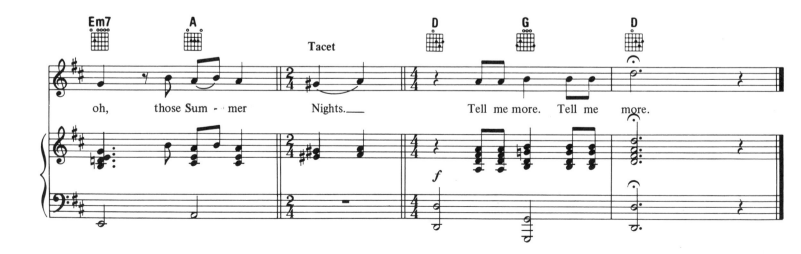

Send in the Clowns
(From the Musical "A LITTLE NIGHT MUSIC")

Music and Lyrics by
STEPHEN SONDHEIM

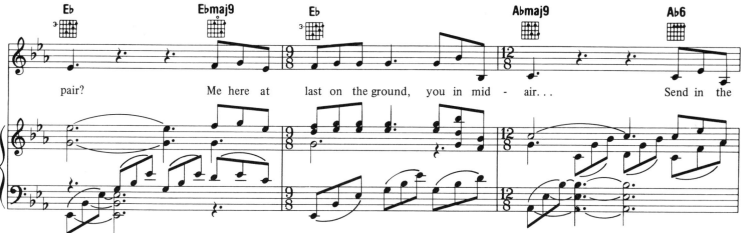

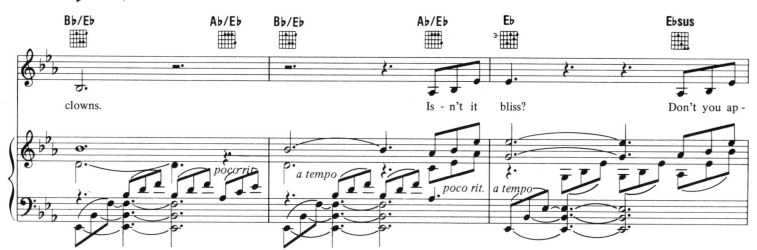

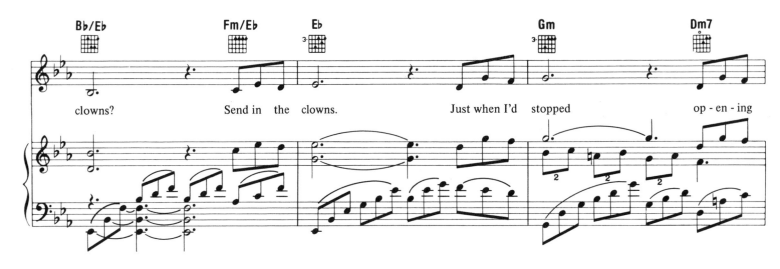

clowns? Send in the clowns. Just when I'd stopped op - en - ing

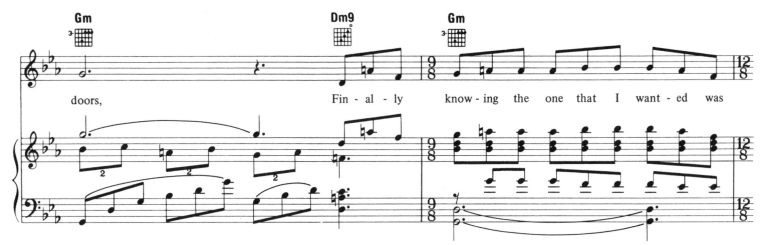

doors, Fin - al - ly know - ing the one that I want - ed was

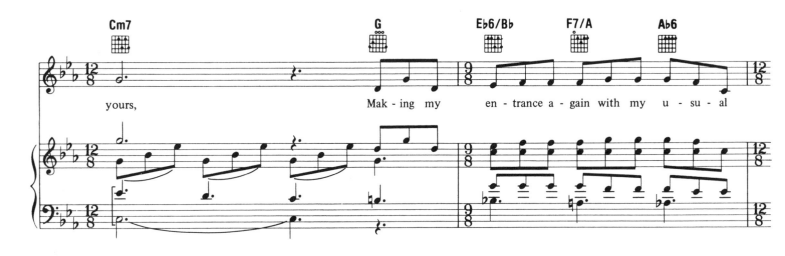

yours, Mak - ing my en - trance a - gain with my u - su - al

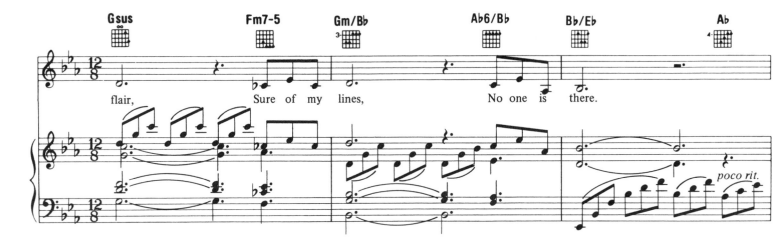

flair, Sure of my lines, No one is there.

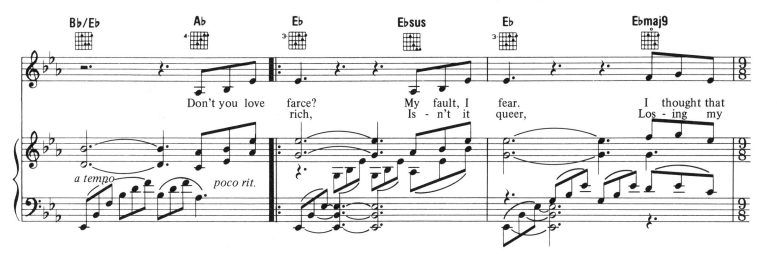

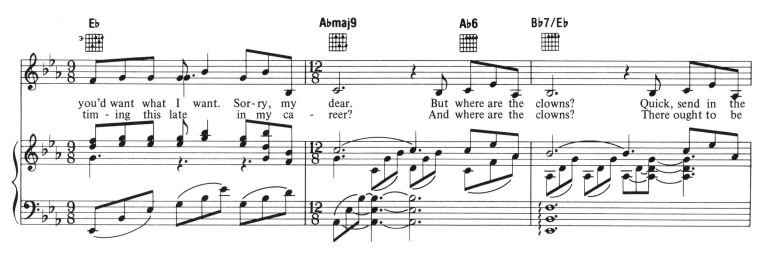

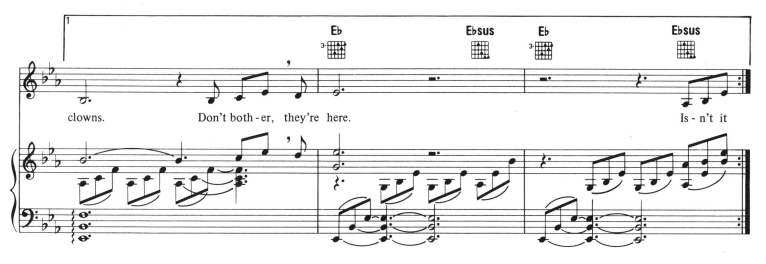

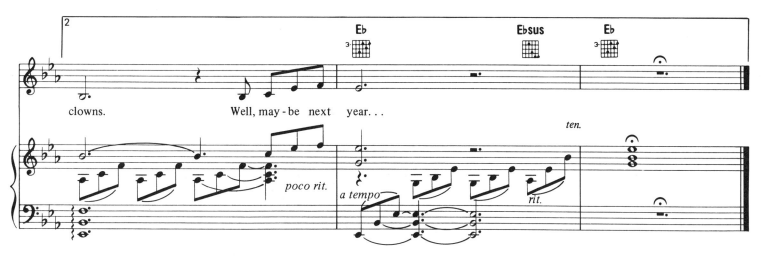

AND ALL THAT JAZZ
(FROM "CHICAGO")

Words by FRED EBB
Music by JOHN KANDER

One

(From "A CHORUS LINE")

Music by MARVIN HAMLISCH
Lyric by EDWARD KLEBAN

From the Joseph Papp Production of Michael Bennett's "A CHORUS LINE"

WHAT I DID FOR LOVE

Music by MARVIN HAMLISCH
Lyric by EDWARD KLEBAN

What I did for love,_____ What I did for_____ love._____

NC Look, my eyes___ are dry,_____ the gift was ours to (dream)

bor - row._____ It's as if___ we al - ways

knew,_____ But I won't for-get _____ What I did for love,-

What I did for love.

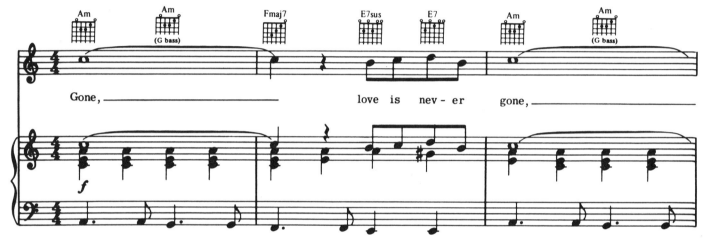

Gone, love is nev - er gone,

As we tra - vel on, love's what we'll re -

mem - ber. Kiss to-day good-bye,

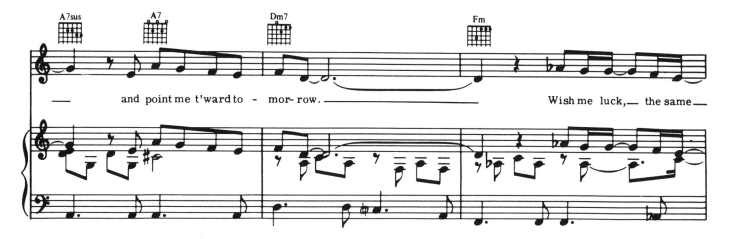

and point me t'ward to - mor - row. _____ Wish me luck, ___ the same ___

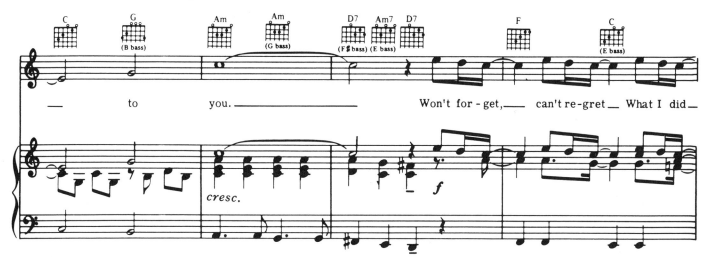

___ to you. _____ Won't for - get, ___ can't re-gret ___ What I did ___

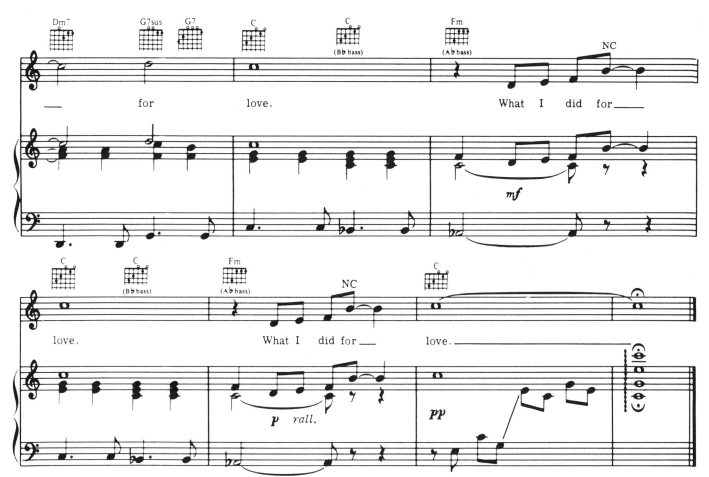

___ for love. What I did for ___ love. What I did for ___ love. ___

TOMORROW
(From "ANNIE")

Lyric by MARTIN CHARNIN
Music by CHARLES STROUSE

IN A SIMPLE WAY I LOVE YOU

Lyrics by GRETCHEN CRYER
Music by NANCY FORD

OLD FRIEND

Lyrics by GRETCHEN CRYER
Music by NANCY FORD

54

DON'T CRY FOR ME ARGENTINA
(From the opera "EVITA")

Lyric by TIM RICE
Music by ANDREW LLOYD WEBBER

Slowly

mp

C   F/C

It won't be ea-sy, you'll think it strange   When I

G7/C

try to ex-plain how I feel,   That I still need your love af-ter

C   Am/C

all that I've done: _____ You won't be-lieve me All you will see is a

So I chose free - dom Run - ning a - round try - ing ev - 'ry - thing new, but noth - ing im - pressed me at all, I nev - er ex - pect - ed it to. Don't cry for me Ar - gen - ti - na_____ the truth is I nev - er left you. All through my

all you have to do is look at me to know that ev - 'ry word is true.

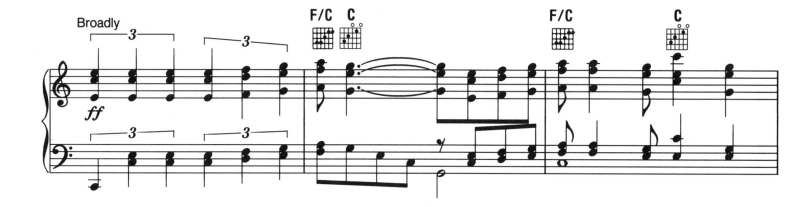

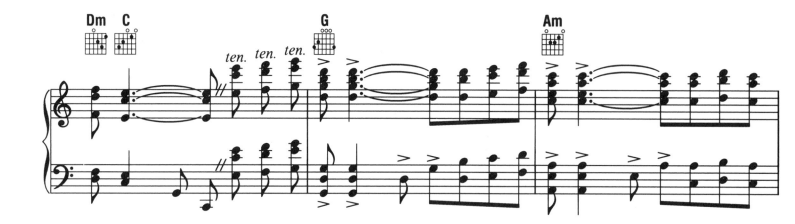

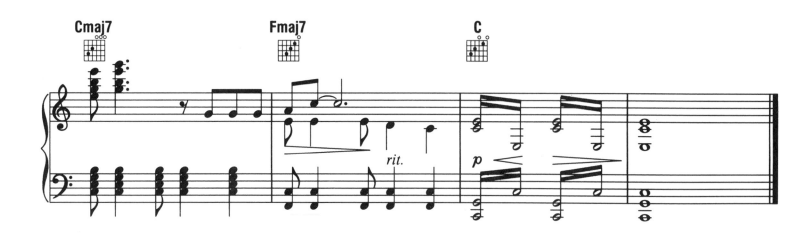

NOT WHILE I'M AROUND

Lyrics and Music by
STEPHEN SONDHEIM

Allegretto (♩ = 176)

mf sempre legato

Not to wor - ry, not to wor - ry, I may not be smart, but I ain't dumb. Let me do it, put me to it, show me some-thing I can o - ver-come. Not to wor - ry,

rit.

PRETTY WOMEN
(From "SWEENEY TODD")

Words and Music by
STEPHEN SONDHEIM

68

Pret - ty wom-en, ___ pret-ty wom - en! ___ Blow-ing out their

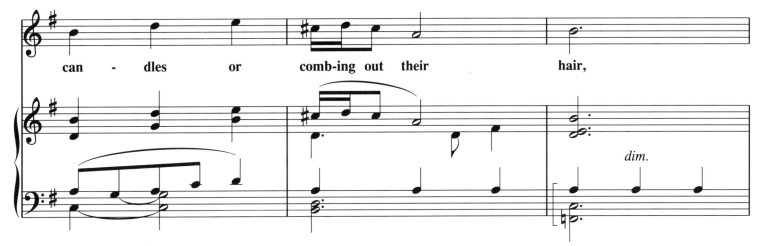

can - dles or comb-ing out their hair,

e - ven when they ___ leave, ___ they still ___ are

there. They're there. Ah,

Pret - ty wom - en at their mir - rors, in their gar - dens, let - ter writ - ing, flow - er pick - ing, weath - er watch - ing,

mf

L.H.

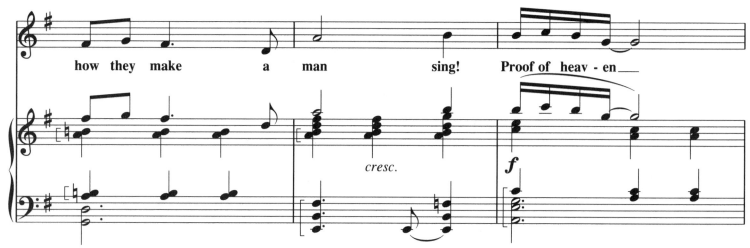

how they make a man sing! Proof of heav - en

cresc. *f*

as you're liv - ing. _ Pret - ty wom - en! _ Yes, pret - ty wom - en! _ Here's to

pret - ty wom - en, pret - ty wom - en, pret - ty wom - en, pret - ty wom - en! _

ff *morendo*

THEY'RE PLAYING MY SONG

(From "THEY'RE PLAYING OUR SONG")

Words by CAROLE BAYER SAGER
Music by MARVIN HAMLISCH

Ho, ho, they're play-ing my song;___ oh, yeah, they're play-ing my song___ and when they're play-ing my song ev-'ry bod-y's got-ta sh, sh, sh. Don't say a word___ now, lis-ten to that sweet mel-o-dy.___ I'm hap-py to say,___ in my

8ba

IF YOU REALLY KNEW ME

Words by CAROLE BAYER SAGER
Music by MARVIN HAMLISCH

Softly, sensitively

mp

If you* real-ly knew_ me, if you real-ly, tru-ly knew_ me,

may-be you would see the oth-er side of me_____ I sel-dom see._

* Female singers may substitute "he" whenever "you" appears.
  Male singers may substitute "she" whenever "you" appears.

If there was no mu - sic, if your mel - o - dy ___ stopped play - ing,

would you be the kind of man (girl) I'd want to see ___ to - night? ___ Does the man (girl) ___

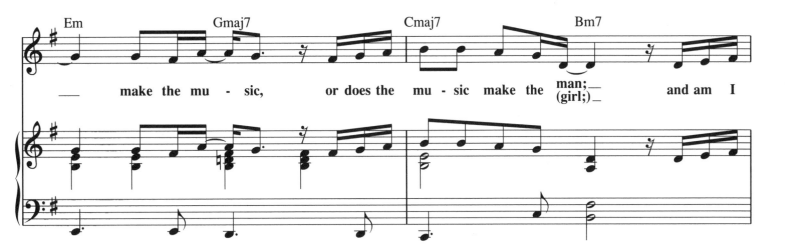

___ make the mu - sic, or does the mu - sic make the man; (girl;) ___ and am I

ev - 'ry - thing ___ I thought I'd be? ___

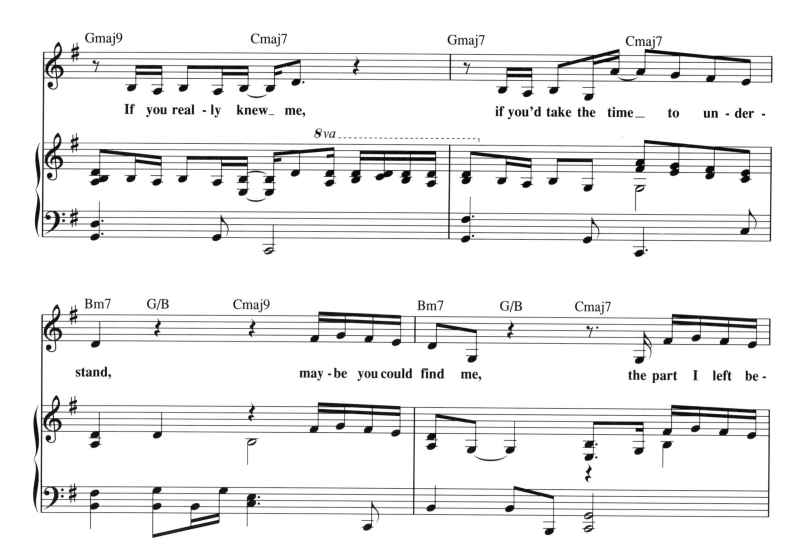

If you real - ly knew_ me, if you'd take the time_ to un - der -

stand, may - be you could find me, the part I left be -

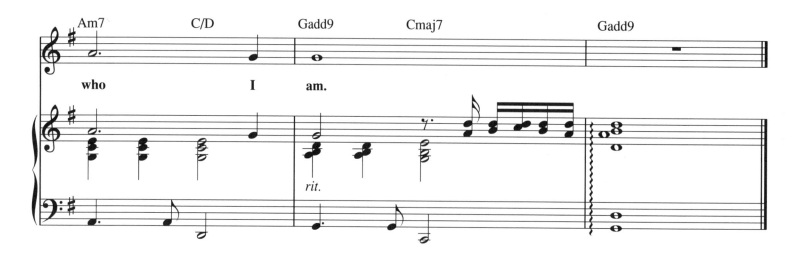

hind me, may - be you'd re - mind me of

who I am.

MEMORY
(From "CATS")

Music by ANDREW LLOYD WEBBER
Text by TREVOR NUNN after T.S. Eliot

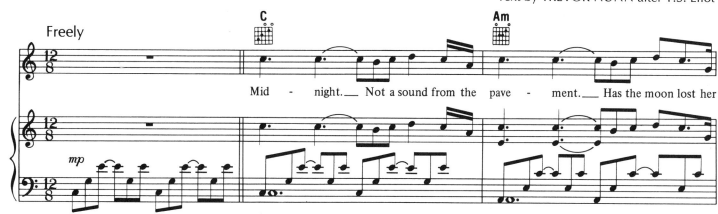

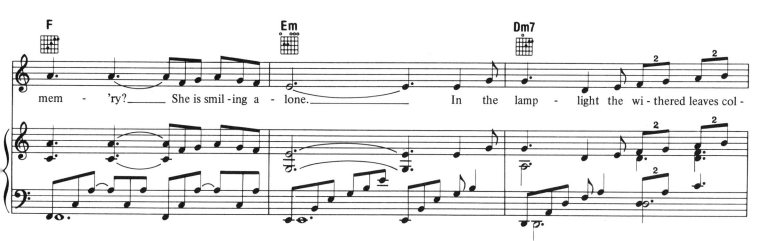

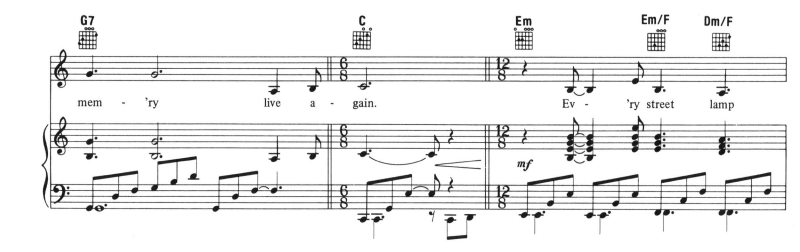

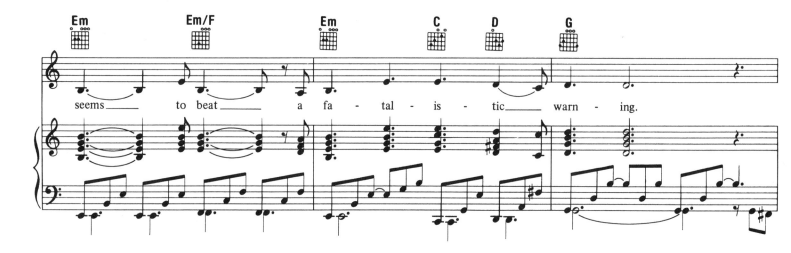

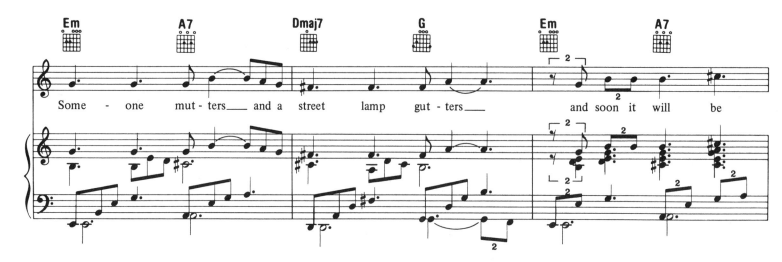

THE BEST OF TIMES

(From the Broadway Musical "La Cage Aux Folles")

Music and Lyric by
JERRY HERMAN

Simply

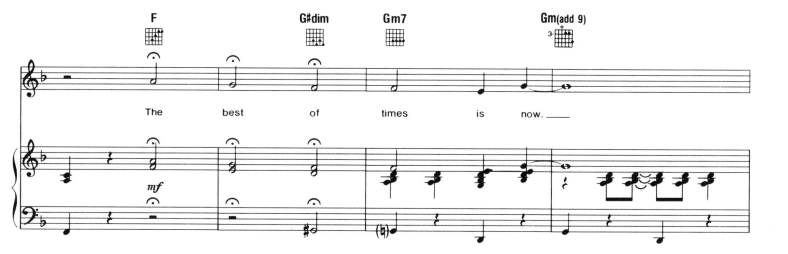

The best of times is now.

What's left of sum-mer but a fad-ed rose? ___

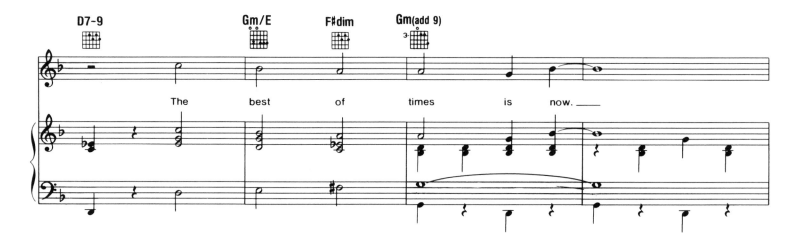

The best of times is now. ___

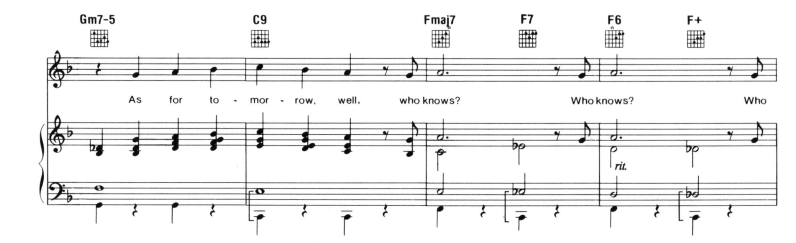

As for to - mor - row, well, who knows? Who knows? Who

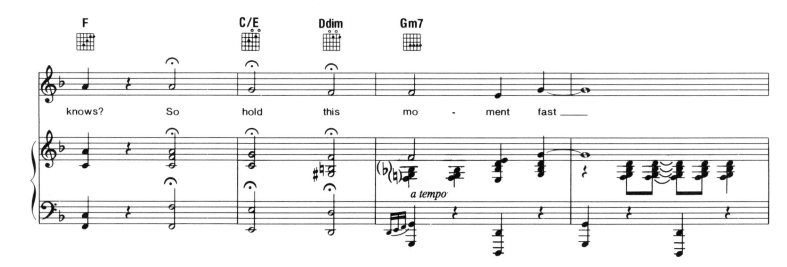

knows? So hold this mo - ment fast ___

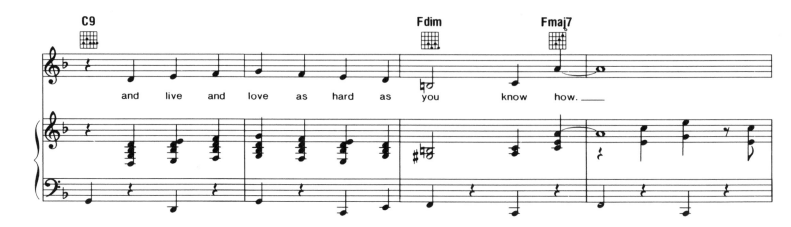

and live and love as hard as you know how. ___

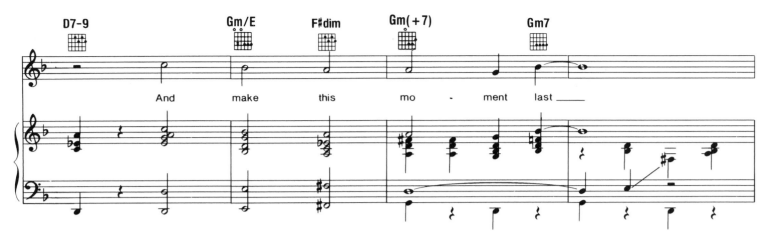

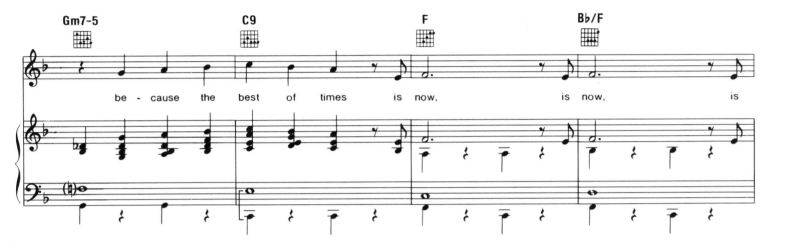

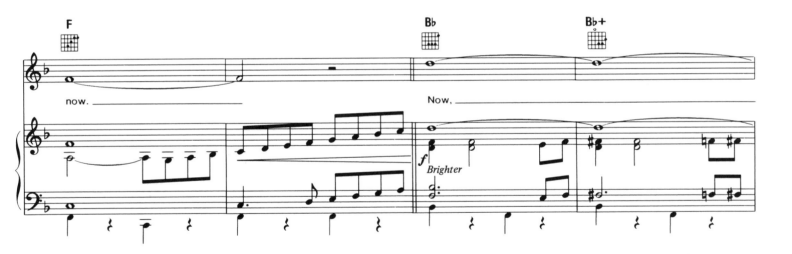

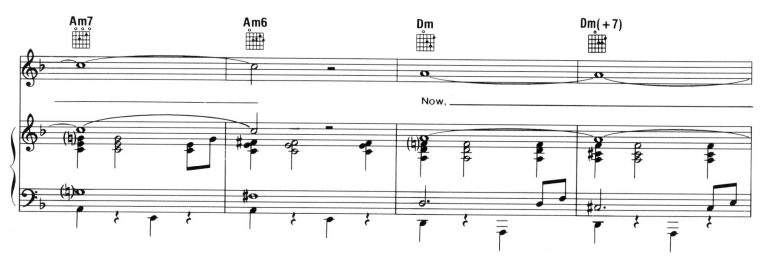

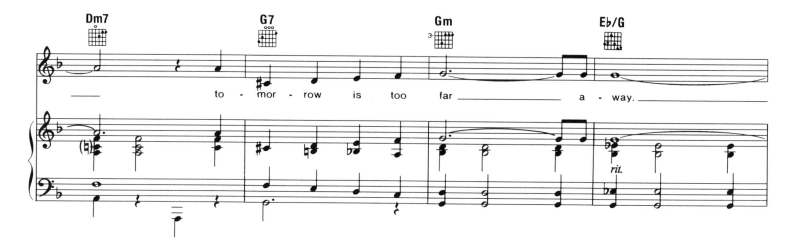

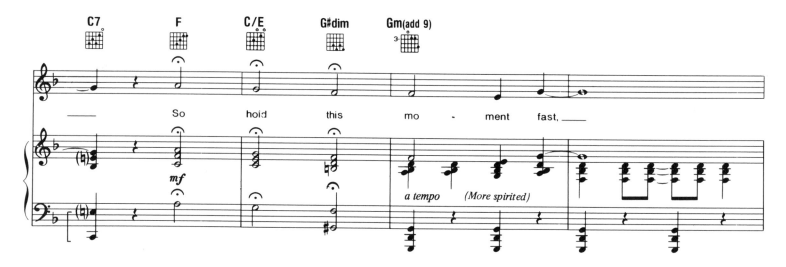

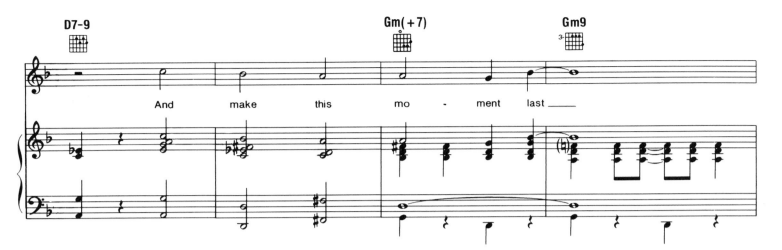

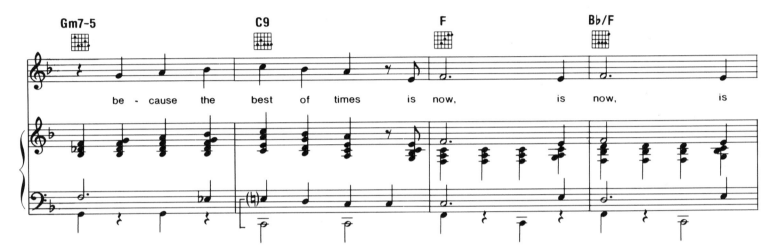

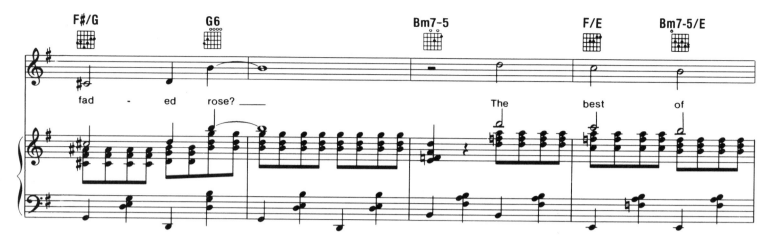

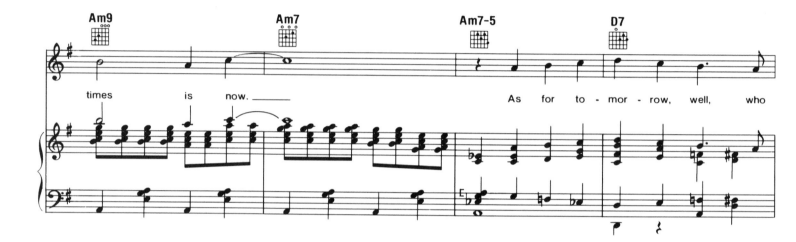

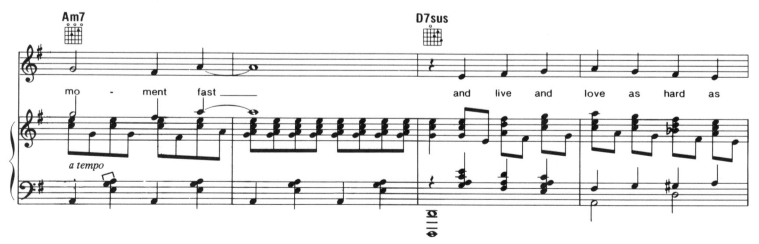

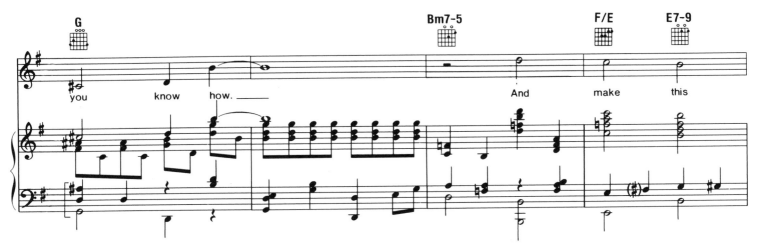

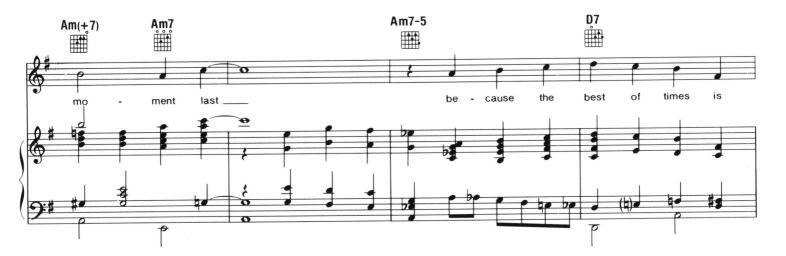

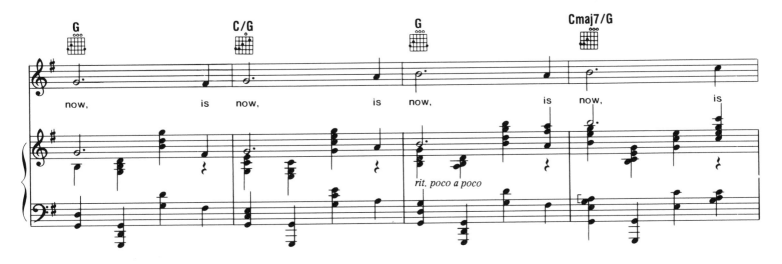

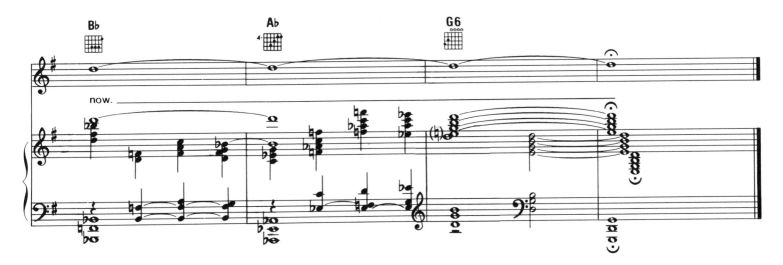

SONG ON THE SAND

(LA DA DA DA)

(From the Broadway musical "La Cage Aux Folles")

Music and Lyric by
JERRY HERMAN

Wistfully

Do you re-call that wind-y lit-tle beach we walked a-long? That af-ter-noon in fall, that af-ter-noon we met? A fel-la with a con-cer-ti-na sang; what was the song? It's strange what we re-call, and

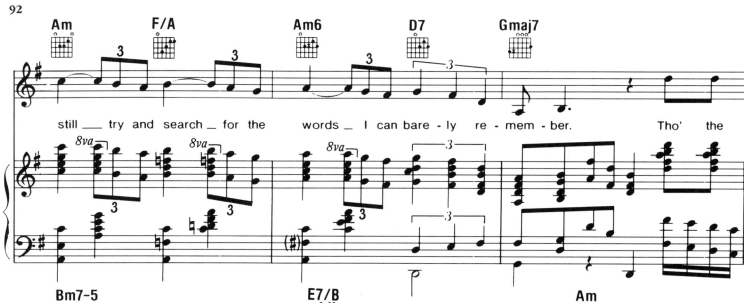

still __ try and search __ for the words __ I can bare - ly re - mem - ber. Tho' the

time __ tum -bles by, __ there is one __ thing that I __ am for - ev - er cer - tain

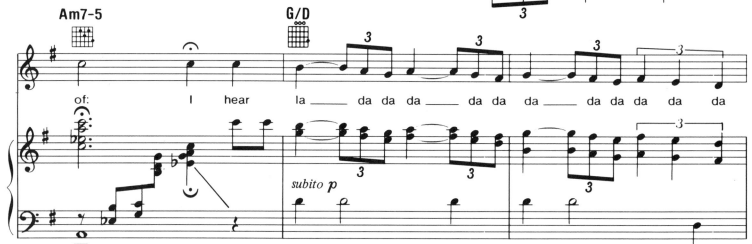

of: I hear la __ da da da __ da da da __ da da da da da

da, and I'm young and in love. __

I AM WHAT I AM

From the Broadway musical "La Cage Aux Folles"

Music and Lyric by
JERRY HERMAN

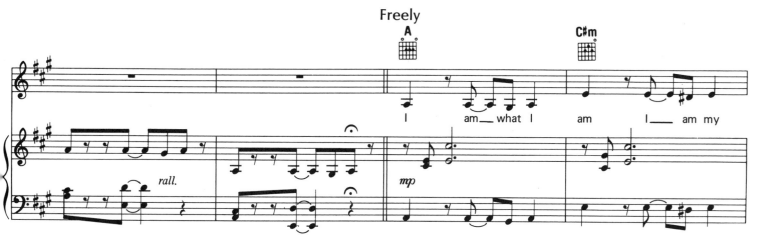

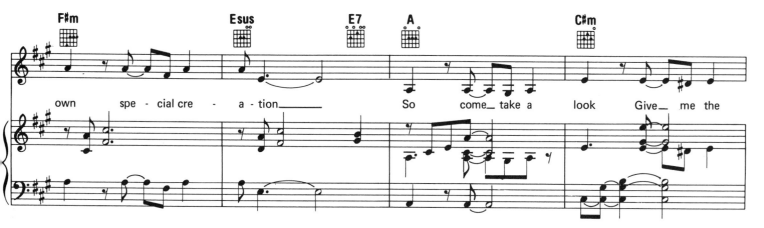

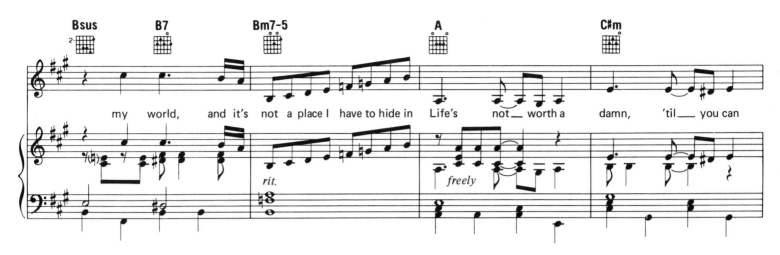

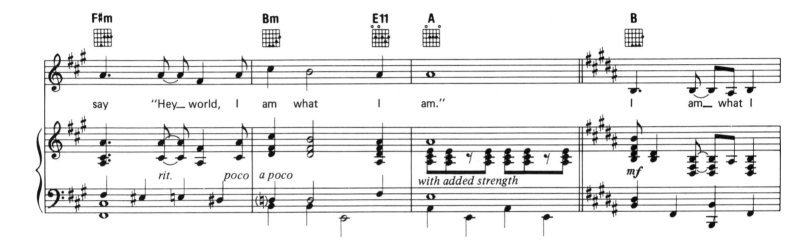

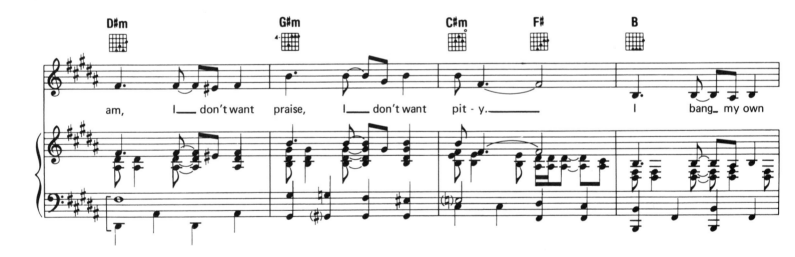

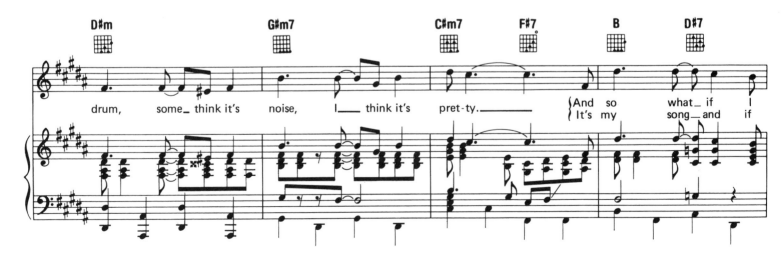

love each feath-er and each span-gle, why not__ try and see things from a diff'-rent an-gle?
you don't like the style I bring it My song,__ so at least re-spect my right to sing it,

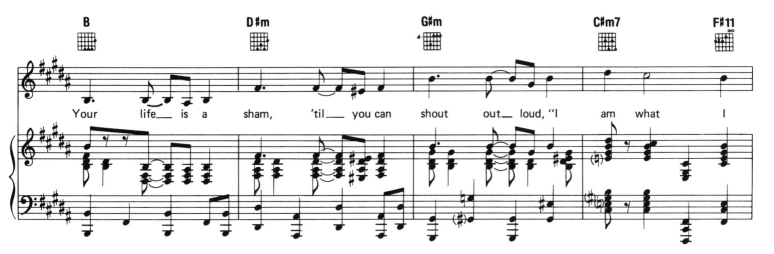

Your life__ is a sham, 'til__ you can shout out__ loud, "I am what I

Twice as Fast

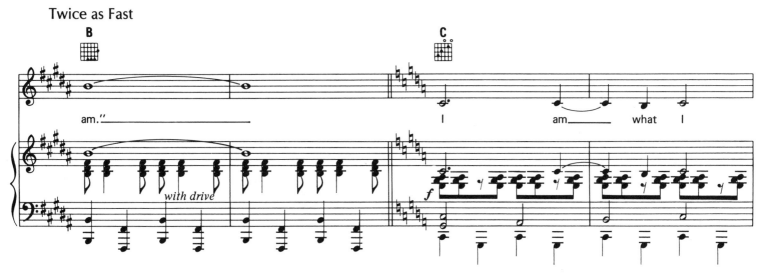

am."__ I am_____ what I

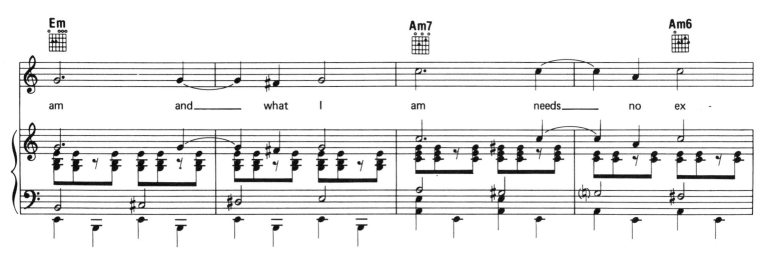

am and_____ what I am needs_____ no ex -

96

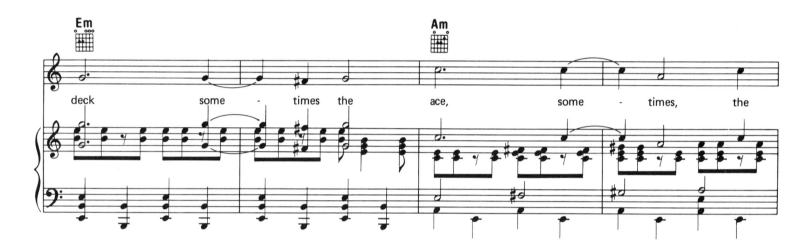

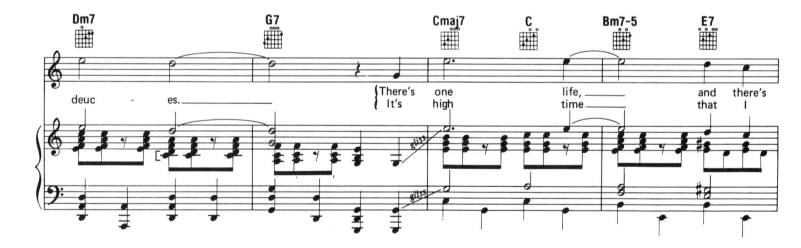

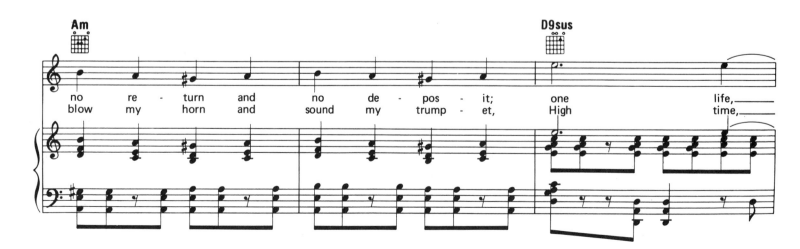

DANCING IS EVERYTHING

Words by ROBERT LORICK
Music by HENRY KRIEGER

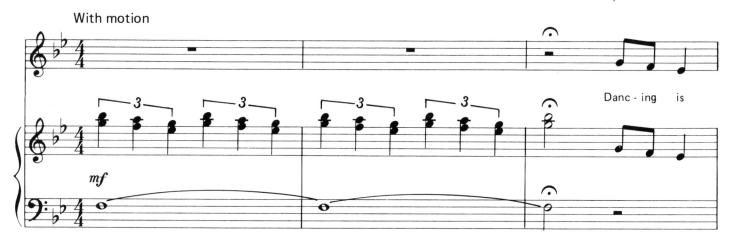

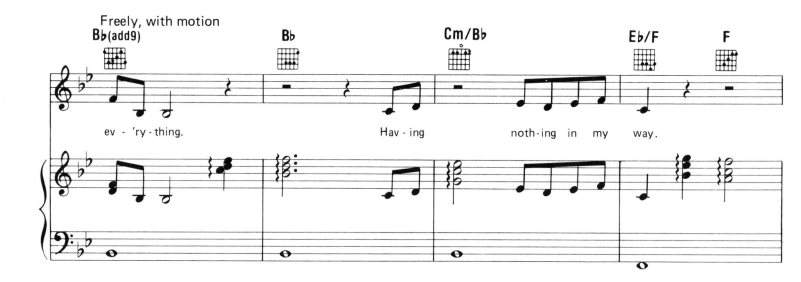

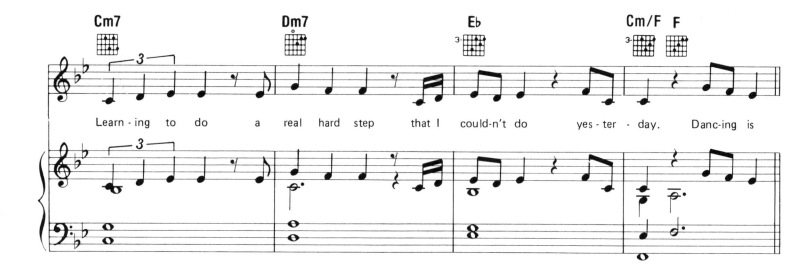

RIVER IN THE RAIN
(From "BIG RIVER")

Music and Lyrics by
ROGER MILLER

Slow

104

TELL ME ON A SUNDAY

Lyrics by DON BLACK
Music by ANDREW LLOYD WEBBER

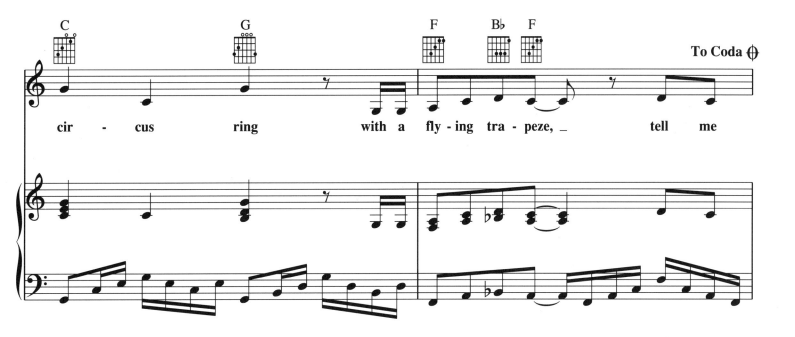

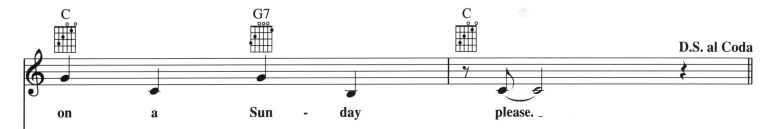

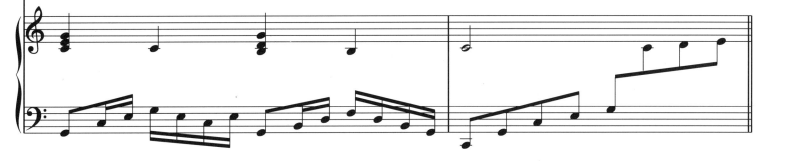

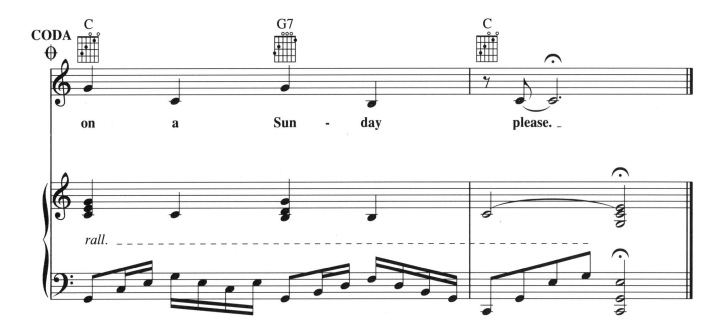

ME AND MY GIRL

Words by DOUGLAS FURBER
Music by NOEL GAY

LAMBETH WALK
(From "ME AND MY GIRL")

Words by DOUGLAS FURBER
Music by NOEL GAY

Moderate 2-beat

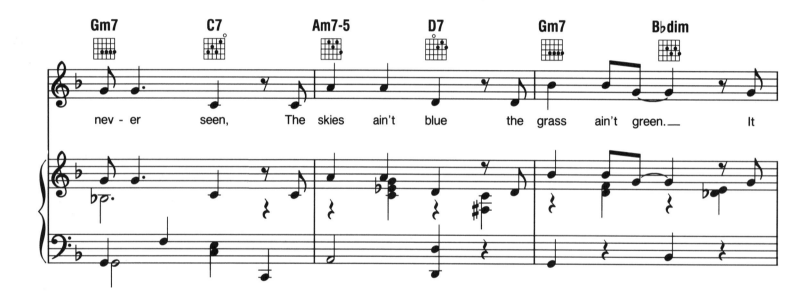

Lam - beth you've nev - er seen, The skies ain't blue the grass ain't green.— It

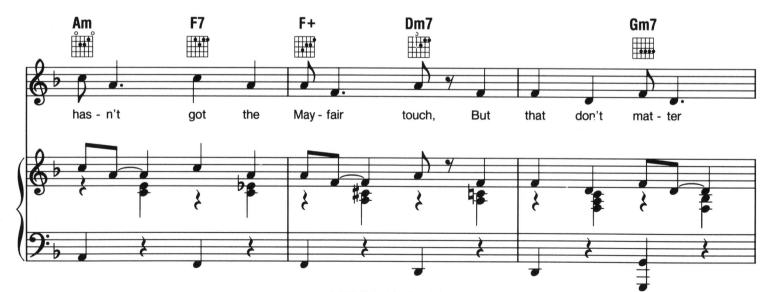

has - n't got the May - fair touch, But that don't mat - ter

LEANING ON A LAMP-POST
(From "ME AND MY GIRL")

Moderately, with a lilting swing (♩♩ played as ⌐³¬♩ ♪)

Words and Music by
NOEL GAY

Lean - ing on a lamp, May-be you think I look a tramp, Or you may think I'm hang-ing 'round to steal a car._____ But no, I'm not a crook, And if you think that's what I look, I'll tell you

I DREAMED A DREAM
(From "LES MISERABLES")

Lyrics by HERBERT KRETZMER
Original Text by ALAIN BOUBLIL & JEAN-MARC NATEL
Music by CLAUDE-MICHEL SCHONBERG

ON MY OWN
(From "LES MISERABLES")

Lyrics by ALAIN BOUBLIL, HERBERT KRETZMER,
JOHN CAIRD, TREVOR NUNN & JEAN- MARC NATEL
Music by CLAUDE-MICHEL SCHONBERG

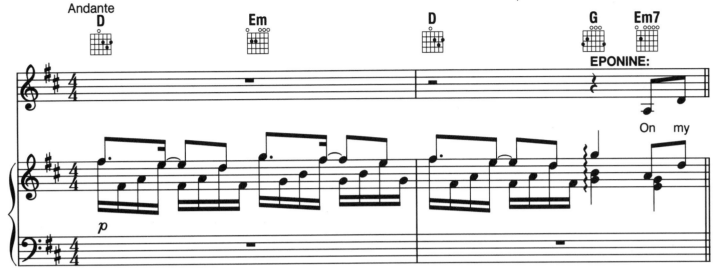

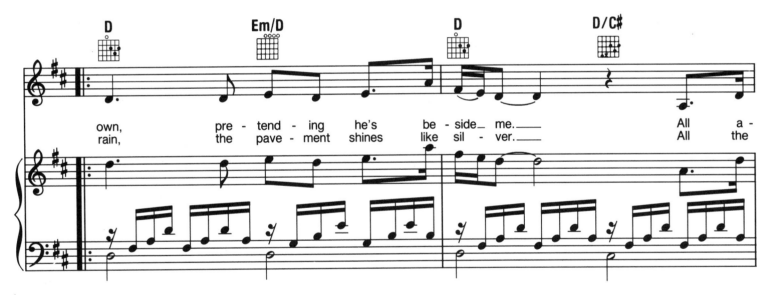

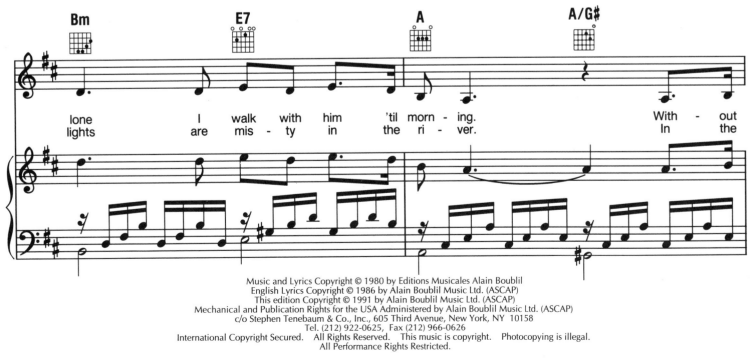

129

MAKE UP MY HEART

Words by RICHARD STILGOE
Music by ANDREW LLOYD WEBBER

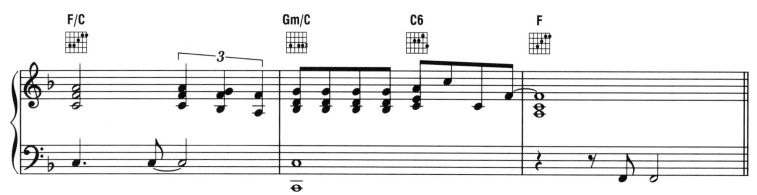

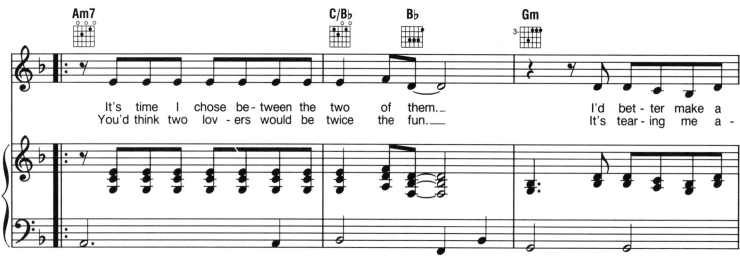

It's time I chose be-tween the two of them.____ I'd bet-ter make a

You'd think two lov-ers would be twice the fun.____ It's tear-ing me a-

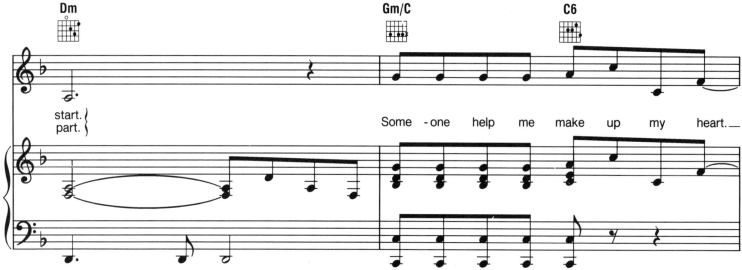

start. part.

Some-one help me make up my heart.____

STARLIGHT EXPRESS
(From "STARLIGHT EXPRESS")

Lyrics by RICHARD STILGOE
Music by ANDREW LLOYD WEBBER

When the night is dark - est,_ o - pen up your mind,

the dream be - gins_ it's be - com - ing clear - er._ Lis - ten to the dis - tance, _ lis-ten and you'll find the mid-night train is get-ting near - er.____

Star - light Ex - press,____ Star - light Ex - press,____ are you real? Yes__ or

no?____ Star - light Ex - press,____ an - swer me "yes."____ I

don't want you__ to go.____ Take me to the pla - ces__

THE MUSIC OF THE NIGHT

Music by ANDREW LLOYD WEBBER
Lyrics by CHARLES HART
Additional Lyrics by RICHARD STILGOE

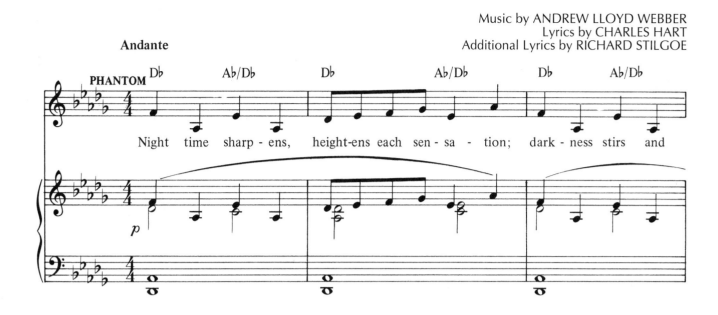

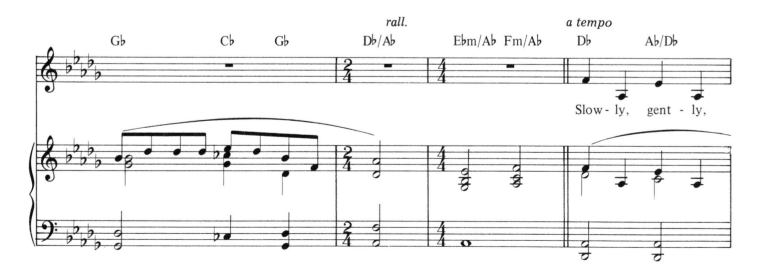

144

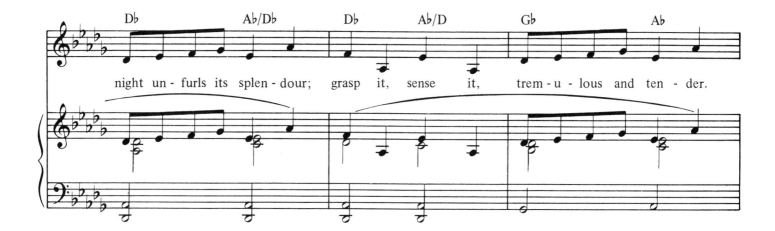

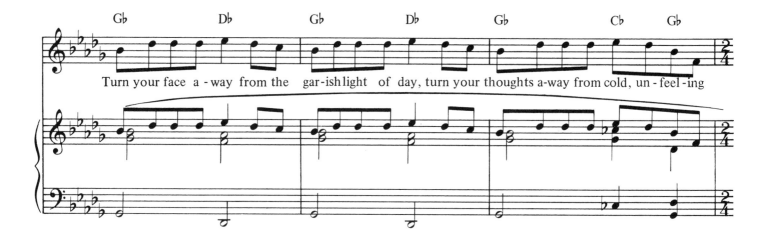

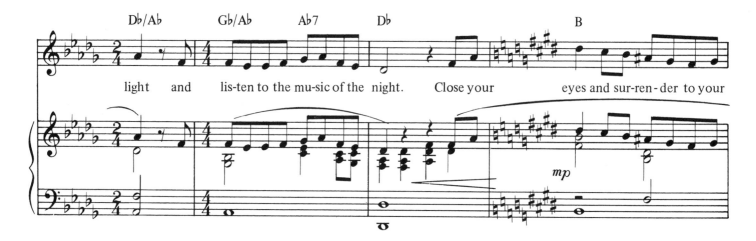

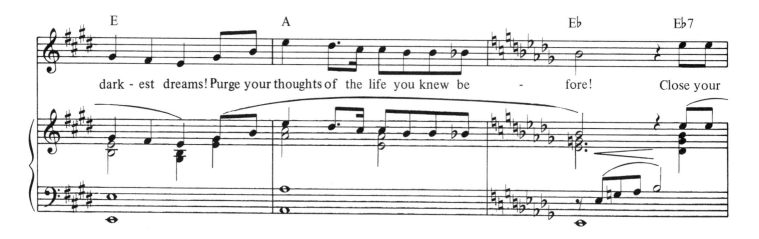

eyes let your spi-rit start to soar and you'll live as you've nev-er lived be - fore.

Soft - ly, deft - ly, mu - sic shall ca - ress you. Hear it, feel it,

se - cret - ly po - ssess you. O - pen up your mind, let your fan - ta - sies un-wind in this

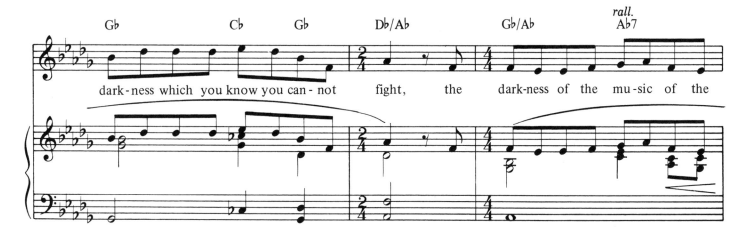

dark-ness which you know you can - not fight, the dark-ness of the mu-sic of the

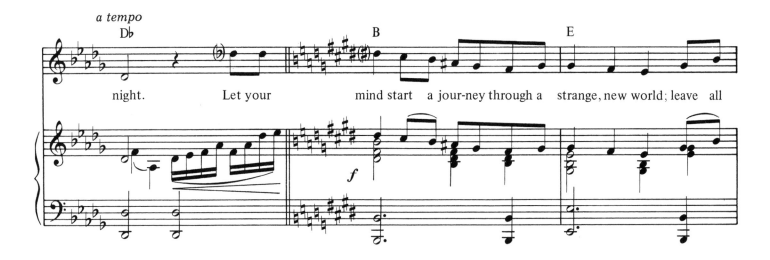

night.   Let your   mind start a jour-ney through a   strange, new world; leave   all

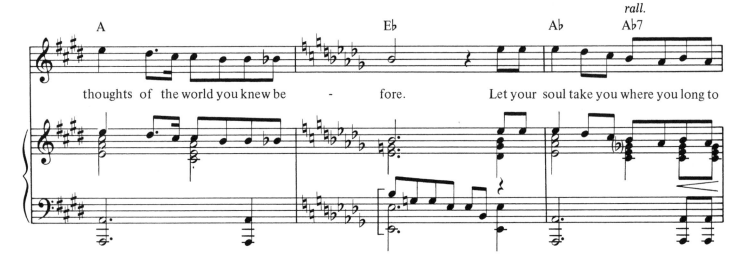

thoughts of the world you knew be -   fore.   Let your soul take you where you long to

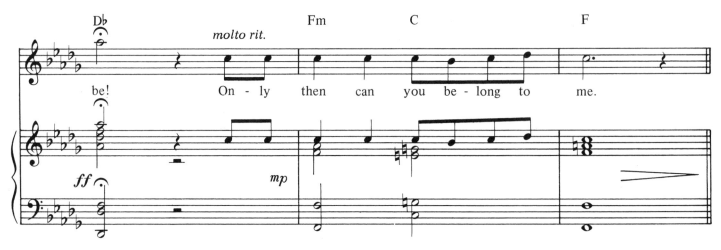

be!   On - ly   then   can   you be - long to   me.

Float -ing,   fall - ing,   sweet in-tox - i - ca - tion.   Touch me, trust   me,   sa-vour each sen-sa - tion.

Let the dream be-gin, let your dark-er side give in to the pow-er of the mu-sic that I write, the

pow-er of the mu-sic of the night.

You a-lone can make my song take

flight, help me make the mu-sic of the night. _____

ANGEL OF MUSIC

Music by ANDREW LLOYD WEBBER
Lyrics by CHARLES HART
Additional Lyrics by RICHARD STILGOE

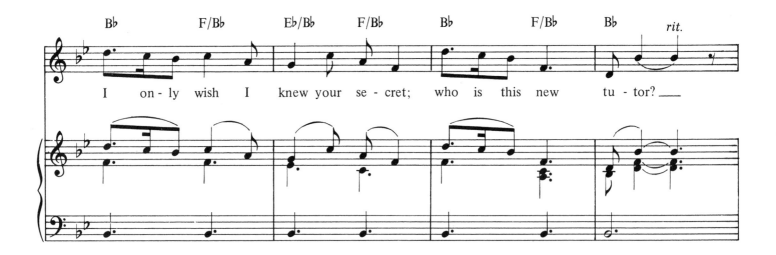

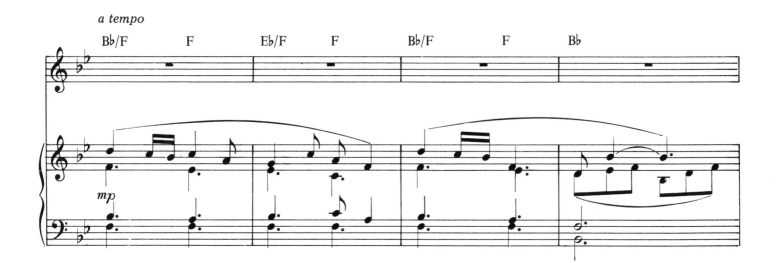

CHRISTINE

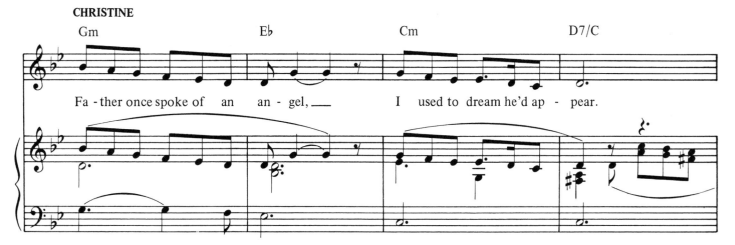

Fa-ther once spoke of an an-gel, __ I used to dream he'd ap - pear.

Now as I sing I can sense him __ and I know he's here.

Here in this room he calls me soft-ly, some-where in-side hid - ing. __

Some-how I know he's al - ways with me; he, the un-seen gen - ius. __

MEG
I watched your face from the shad- ows___ dis-tant through all the ap - plause.
I hear your voice in the dark - ness,___ yet the words aren't yours.

CHRISTINE
An - gel of mu - sic, guide and guar-dian, grant to me your glo-ry!___
CHRISTINE
MEG Who is this an -gel, this

an - gel of mu - sic, hide no long- er, se - cret and strange an-gel.___ He's
CHRISTINE

152

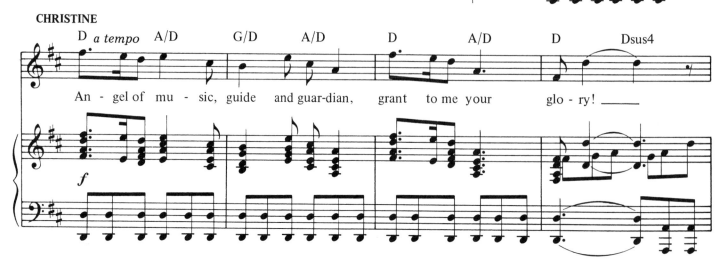

153

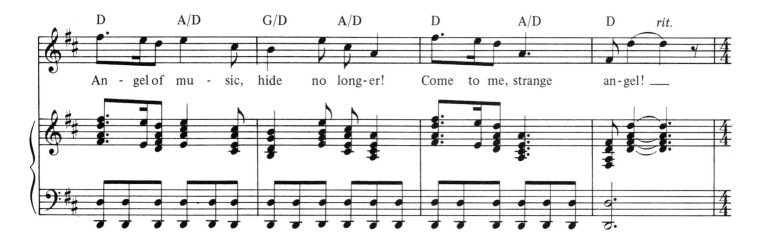

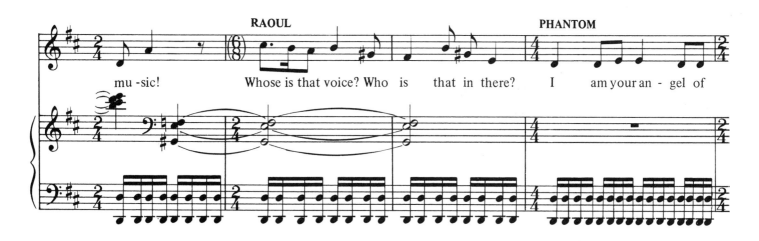

ALL I ASK OF YOU

Music by ANDREW LLOYD WEBBER
Lyrics by CHARLES HART
Additional Lyrics by RICHARD STILGOE

No more talk of dark-ness, for-get these wide-eyed fears; I'm

here, noth-ing can harm you, my words will warm and calm you.

Let me be your free-dom, let day-light dry your tears; I'm

here, with you, be-side you, to guard you and to guide you.

CHRISTINE

All I ask is ev-ery wak-ing mo-ment, turn my head with talk of

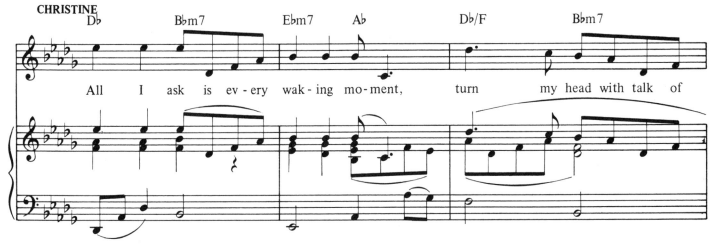

sum-mer-time.__ Say you need me with you now and al-ways;

pro-mise me that all you say is true, that's all I ask of

156

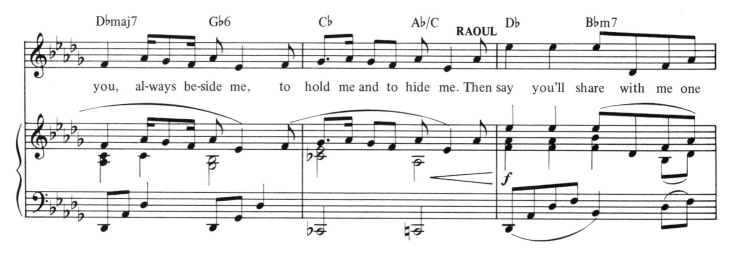

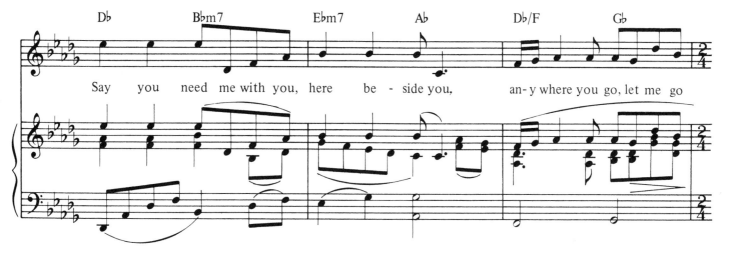

Say you need me with you, here be - side you, an-y where you go, let me go

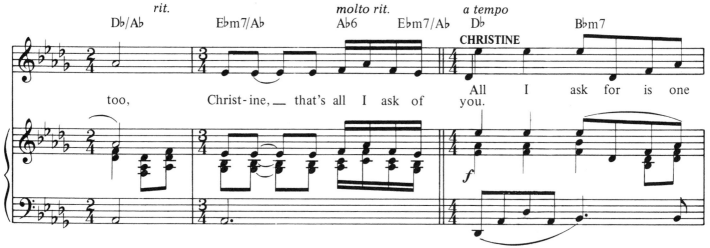

too, Christ-ine,__ that's all I ask of you. **CHRISTINE** All I ask for is one

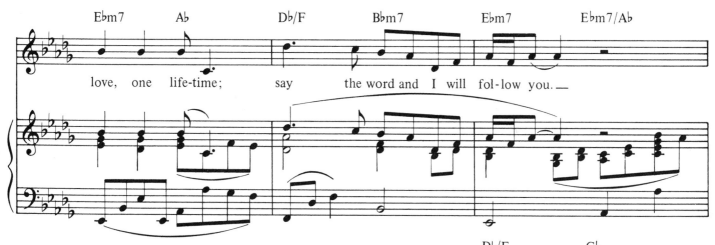

love, one life-time; say the word and I will fol-low you.__

TOGETHER Share each day with me, each night, each morn-ing. **CHRISTINE** Say you love me! **RAOUL** You know I

158

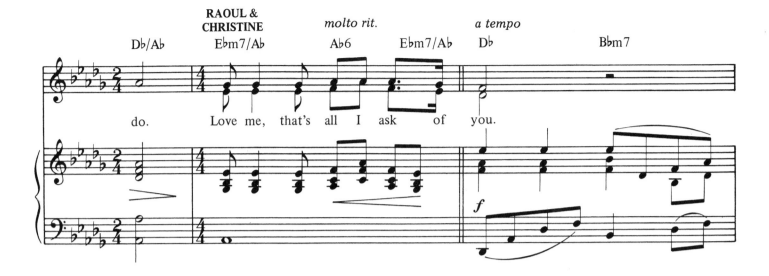

BROADWAY MUSICALS
Show by Show

BROADWAY MUSICALS SHOW BY SHOW 1891 - 1916

33 CLASSICS FROM SHOWS SUCH AS: *ROBIN HOOD, FLORODORA, BABES IN TOYLAND, THE MERRY WIDOW,* AND MORE. SONGS INCLUDE: AFTER THE BALL • THE BOWERY • GIVE MY REGARDS TO BROADWAY • I LOVE YOU SO! (THE MERRY WIDOW WALTZ) • THE ISLE OF OUR DREAMS • KISS ME AGAIN • MARCH OF THE TOYS • MARY'S A GRAND OLD NAME • MY HERO • SIMPLE MELODY • STREETS OF NEW YORK • TOYLAND • AND MORE.
00311514 $12.95

BROADWAY MUSICALS SHOW BY SHOW 1917 - 1929

OVER 40 SONGS FROM THE ERA'S MOST POPULAR SHOWS, INCLUDING: *ZIEGFELD FOLLIES, THE STUDENT PRINCE IN HEIDELBERG, NO NO NANETTE, OH, KAY!, SHOW BOAT, FIFTY MILLION FRENCHMEN,* AND MORE. SONGS INCLUDE: THE BIRTH OF THE BLUES • CAN'T HELP LOVIN' DAT MAN • FASCINATING RHYTHM • HOW LONG HAS THIS BEEN GOING ON? • I'M JUST WILD ABOUT HARRY • OL' MAN RIVER • A PRETTY GIRL IS LIKE A MELODY • ST. LOUIS BLUES • SECOND HAND ROSE • TEA FOR TWO • YOU DO SOMETHING TO ME • YOU'RE THE CREAM IN MY COFFEE • AND MORE.
00311515 $14.95

THIS UNIQUE SERIES EXPLORES BROADWAY'S BIGGEST HITS·YEAR BY YEAR AND SHOW BY SHOW. INTERESTING FACTS AND TRIVIA AS WELL AS ARRANGEMENTS FOR THE BEST SONGS FROM EACH SHOW ARE PRESENTED IN A PACKAGE NO BROADWAY FAN CAN RESIST! THE TEXT ABOUT THE SHOWS WAS WRITTEN BY RENOWNED BROADWAY HISTORIAN STANLEY GREEN, AND IS DRAWN FROM HIS BOOK *BROADWAY MUSICALS SHOW BY SHOW.* THIS IS DEFINITELY THE ULTIMATE COLLECTION OF BROADWAY MUSIC AND HISTORY — BE SURE TO COLLECT·THE WHOLE SERIES!

BROADWAY MUSICALS SHOW BY SHOW 1950 - 1959

55 SONGS FROM SUCH CLASSICS AS *THE KING AND I, MY FAIR LADY, WEST SIDE STORY, GYPSY, THE SOUND OF MUSIC,* AND MORE. SONGS INCLUDE: DO-RE-MI • EDELWEISS • EVERYTHING'S COMING UP ROSES • GETTING TO KNOW YOU • I COULD HAVE DANCED ALL NIGHT • I'VE GROWN ACCUSTOMED TO HER FACE • LET ME ENTERTAIN YOU • LUCK BE A LADY • MACK THE KNIFE • MARIA • SEVENTY SIX TROMBONES • SHALL WE DANCE? • SOMEWHERE • WOULDN'T IT BE LOVERLY • AND MORE.
00311518 $14.95

BROADWAY MUSICALS SHOW BY SHOW 1960 - 1971

OVER 45 SONGS FROM SHOWS SUCH AS *OLIVER!, CABARET, CAMELOT, HELLO, DOLLY!, FIDDLER ON THE ROOF, JESUS CHRIST SUPERSTAR, MAME,* AND MORE. SONGS INCLUDE: AS LONG AS HE NEEDS ME • CONSIDER YOURSELF • DAY BY DAY • I DON'T KNOW HOW TO LOVE HIM • IF EVER I WOULD LEAVE YOU • IF I WERE A RICH MAN • PEOPLE • SUNRISE, SUNSET • TRY TO REMEMBER • WE NEED A LITTLE CHRISTMAS • WHAT KIND OF FOOL AM I? • AND MORE.
00311521 $14.95

BROADWAY MUSICALS SHOW BY SHOW 1930 - 1939

A COLLECTION OF OVER 45 SONGS FROM THE DECADE'S BIGGEST BROADWAY HITS, INCLUDING: *ANYTHING GOES, PORGY AND BESS, BABES IN ARMS, ON YOUR TOES* AND MORE. SONGS INCLUDE: BEGIN THE BEGUINE • EMBRACEABLE YOU • FALLING IN LOVE WITH LOVE • FRIENDSHIP • I GET A KICK OUT OF YOU • I GOT RHYTHM • THE LADY IS A TRAMP • MY FUNNY VALENTINE • MY HEART BELONGS TO DADDY • ON YOUR TOES • SMOKE GETS IN YOUR EYES • STRIKE UP THE BAND • SUMMERTIME • IT AIN'T NECESSARILY SO • AND MORE.
00311516 $14.95

BROADWAY MUSICALS SHOW BY SHOW 1940 - 1949

SHOW DESCRIPTIONS AND OVER 45 SONGS FROM THE BROADWAY HITS *PAL JOEY, OKLAHOMA!, CAROUSEL, ANNIE GET YOUR GUN, FINIAN'S RAINBOW, SOUTH PACIFIC* AND MORE. SONGS INCLUDE: ANOTHER OP'NIN, ANOTHER SHOW • BALI HAI • BEWITCHED • DIAMOND'S ARE A GIRL'S BEST FRIEND • IF I LOVED YOU • NEW YORK, NEW YORK • OH, WHAT A BEAUTIFUL MORNIN' • OLD DEVIL MOON • SOME ENCHANTED EVENING • THE SURREY WITH THE FRINGE ON TOP • YOU'LL NEVER WALK ALONE • MORE.
00311517 $14.95

BROADWAY MUSICALS SHOW BY SHOW 1972 - 1988

OVER 30 SONGS FROM THE ERA OF BIG PRODUCTIONS LIKE *PHANTOM OF THE OPERA, EVITA, LA CAGE AUX FOLLES, LES MISERABLES, ME AND MY GIRL, A CHORUS LINE, CATS* AND MORE. SONGS INCLUDE: ALL I ASK OF YOU • DON'T CRY FOR ME ARGENTINA • I AM WHAT I AM • I DREAMED A DREAM • THE LAMBETH WALK • MEMORY • THE MUSIC OF THE NIGHT • ON MY OWN • SEND IN THE CLOWNS • TOMORROW • WHAT I DID FOR LOVE • AND MORE.
00311519 $14.95

Prices, contents and availability subject to change without notice.

For more information, see your local music dealer, or write to:
Hal Leonard Publishing Corporation
P.O. Box 13819 Milwaukee, Wisconsin 53213